Frogs and Snails and Mobster Tales:
Growing up in Al Capone's Shadow

Robert J. Teitelbaum

and

Cindy L. Carter

fight and love

Robert Keitelba

CONTENTS

Foreword

Frogs and Snails and Mobster Tales is the story of one little boy, a courageous survivor who poignantly paints a vivid picture of abuse, neglect, and family dysfunction, including addiction, co-dependency, family conflict, unresolved loss and grief. You will be moved by his resilient nature as he faces many challenges and much adversity with the resources of a child, yet he keeps getting back up every single time that he's knocked down. Little Robert keeps on moving forward, despite all the trauma and turmoil he keeps tucked away inside.

This is truly a book about hope in the most desperate circumstances. Finding a voice, dealing with the trauma and pain, getting help, coming to terms with the huge price paid through the years, making peace with the past, coming to a place of forgiveness - all create the possibility of healing and moving forward.

Robert's wife, Carol Teitelbaum, leads a program called "It Happens to Boys". With a group of male survivors of childhood sexual abuse, they do presentations at conferences, schools and treatment centers, reaching the general public through television, radio, and print interviews. They talk about the problem and the solutions. Participants hear a variety of powerful messages directed specifically to those who've been violated, such as:

It's not your fault. You are not to blame. It's okay to talk about this. Get help for yourself. Find someone safe you can trust.

Currently, Robert often plays an integral part of this process. His participation helps children hear the important messages he never heard as a child. That is a joy in his healing and on-going recovery. Robert's story now shines light on a huge epidemic in our country, one that many find uncomfortable to discuss and others completely overlook - childhood sexual abuse. There are 39 million survivors in the United States and countless more around the world.

The median age of abuse is nine years old. According to the Center for Disease Control and Prevention, one out of every six boys and one out of every four girls are sexually abused during childhood. This atrocity is grossly under-reported, particularly in terms of boys.

Ninety-three percent of these children knew and trusted their perpetrators, forty percent were abused by older or larger children they knew. Most become enveloped in a conspiracy of silence, shame, and secrecy. 'Don't Talk, Don't Trust, and Don't Feel' becomes a mantra to survive each day. These children are robbed of innocence, joy, and childhood. Their spirit is compromised in a pervasive and stifling manner. Self-hate and loathing can rule the day.

From an early age, boys are consistently given messages to be strong, buck up, be a man, don't cry, don't act like a sissy, and don't act like a girl. Boys learn to repress their feelings and emotional pain. Repressed feelings and pain often surface as rage in men. When boys are abused, they feel an enormous amount of shame, typically believing it is their fault because they were not strong enough to protect themselves. This can be true for boys as young as four. The shame and guilt often increase through the years when - as men - they look back, always thinking they were bigger and stronger than they actually were.

If a boy is gay and abused by an adult man, he often thinks he must have somehow wanted the abuse. If a boy is straight and abused by a man, he often is afraid to tell because people will think he is gay. When a boy is sexually abused by a woman, he is more likely to get a high five than empathy. He's also afraid to tell for fear that no one will believe him. No matter what the circumstances might be, a child is not emotionally ready for a sexual experience. When boys are abused, most grow up believing and feeling they are not real men.

Often there is so much anger and nowhere to appropriately deal with it. Some men, carrying all that heavy emotional baggage for years, direct that anger outwardly. Rage, domestic violence, physical and emotional abuse are cycled and recycled in a destructive fashion that never lets up. Others turn inwardly and self-medicate with alcohol, drugs, cutting, and other self-destructive behaviors. Sometimes the pain, shame, and self-hate become so overwhelming that suicide appears the only way out.

While Robert's story emerges from a culture of organized crime, the abuses he sustained are no strangers to many families, whether of upper, middle, or lower socio-economic class origins. Perpetrators walk unrecognized in all social settings. Our best response is approach. Talk with each other. Ask questions and create trust in a safe place where each person, each child can tell their stories, just like Robert does here.

Jerry Moe, National Director, Children's Programs, Betty Ford Center

Introduction

What are little boys made of?
What are little boys made of?
Snips & snails & puppy dogs tails,
And such are little boys made of.
                    From a 19th century nursery rhyme

Dating from the 1800's, this popular nursery rhyme was read to me by my favorite aunt, my mother's sister, Hannah. I begged her to read it to me as often as she would while I was growing up at the Loveless Ranch. Fascinated by every word in this childhood poem, my own childhood was stirred in a cauldron of far less innocent ingredients. The truth is my childhood was short-lived in a family populated with thugs, thieves, bigamists, and even far more serious dangers.

I was born into a colorful family entangled with mobsters who generated more mobsters. My personal history includes graphic details about childhood scenes ripe with physical and emotional blows; recurring patterns of absence, abuse, and neglect. The characters of well-known and less-chronicled mobsters formed my perspectives as a child growing up in the 1940s and 50s; I was clearly an innocent child caught in the middle of extraordinary chaos.

Memories, however personal and intense, are always fragmented; often enough to obscure layers of significance. In my own case, these layers of fragmentation forged the raw material for my ability to survive over the decades, only to work through them later in life while gaining perspectives on my relationships and on the lives of those closest to me. It is helpful to remember that while I lived in the middle of a fishbowl, it was nearly impossible for me to recognize the cloudy waters; our polluted environment simply appeared natural to me.

Stories, by their very nature, reflect the storyteller's inner world of perceptions that are, in truth, personal images and feelings about both real and imagined events. Stories do not represent indisputable truths about any single event, rather they retell events remembered in the storyteller's mind. These principles are particularly true about the stories chronicled in this book.

Each of the events involving family members and other characters retold in this book are drawn from my personal experience and may or may not bear any resemblance to those same events recalled by others. What follows is not intended to represent objective truth, rather it represents my own personal truths, which I stand by even as I bear testimonial scars to those memories. Out of respect, names of certain friends and family members have been changed to protect others' integrity and privacy.

'Frogs and Snails and Mobster Tales' reveals my observations about a particularly challenging childhood; it shines a bright light on the need for a culture of responsible and compassionate child-care. Like the sentiments of the campfire song, 'You are My Sunshine', every one of us bears the responsibility to shine a bright protective light on our children's safety.

As the years passed from childhood to adulthood, I began to hear the personal stories of other family members who were affected by much of the same abuse to which I was subjected, some greater and some less so. I heard other family stories that made me laugh. Together, these stories began to bridge the fragmentations and awaken many long-buried memories, both in images and feelings, bringing slivers of clarity and integrity to my own story.

After some time of trying to sort through these images and emotions I realized that I should seek help to enlighten the past and to help structure the stories in my own mind; to learn to look beyond the obvious events as I recalled them and add perspective to the human dynamics that shaped me growing up. A friend and I agreed to drop into those historic deeply hidden canyons together as writing partners. We were guided by intuition, compassion, courage, legal documents, eyewitness accounts, and relentless attention to intimate detail as we entered this exploration together.

The story of my life was buried under years of well-integrated coping mechanisms. Recovery required sifting through piles of rubble, sorting out images, feelings, facts and curiosities; it required patience, perseverance, tenderness, and, sometimes forced while other times easy optimism. My writing partner's participation was offered without reservation. She heard me say that I needed help and reminded me that a friend shows up when help is needed. She helped birth the stories by witnessing each detail, each emotion, and even each missing element.

With a background in psychology and academia, my partner's expertise dovetailed with my own family history and storytelling traditions to create a new story; a story rich with important lessons about the human spirit. My journey challenges others to look forward and backward, thinking critically not just about their own lives but also about the well-being of others. Both my writing partner and I were deeply changed as we navigated through these dark canyons together.

My wife Carol's enduring love for me and for others is the rich soil upon which I continue to thrive. Before we married, Carol already knew about my dark family history. Additionally, my sisters confided in Carol about some of their own torturous childhood experiences. Despite these revelations, both sisters and I continued to use drugs and alcohol to keep our rage at bay over several decades of anguish.

Thirty years after the abuse ended, Carol facilitated a sibling confrontation, including our mother and brother. The result was that my sisters and I drew closer to each other while our mother and brother, who remained in denial, detached further from us. Our mother at age 85 refused to give up her relationship with our primary perpetrator, which deeply grieved us, while our brother just moved as far away from us as he could.

This book could not have been written without the loving trust offered whole-heartedly by Carol. She has a gentle strength that encourages me to listen, challenge myself, reflect on life, and tap enough courage to uncover a haunting story. Carol is a guide to many in the underworld of fears.

Both of my sisters inspired this book by their own writings and stories. Knowing the truth about their childhoods convinced me that children need to be protected and their behavior needs to be understood. If writing this story any sooner could have helped save my sisters' grief, I would have done it.

Many of my cousins still carry 'family secrets' and a fair amount of pain. My love for them is strong enough for me to model a new approach to family secrets, one that releases the agony of maintaining horrible stories held within tightly clenched fists.

One cousin in particular, Roger, has been my story-telling companion. As a direct witness, he also confronted many of his own family memories; we catalyzed each other's work. His academic expertise breathed new life into this book.

My childhood is recorded chronologically. If the story sequence feels disorienting to readers, my early life experiences have been accurately conveyed. Life rotated around the dizzying presence of innocence, pain, creativity, confusion, danger, love, loss, and desire. There were few opportunities to develop trust or any expectations whatsoever, other than in the pervasive company of danger and chaos.

It's finally clear that childhood demons can be released through written words, making room for healthy experiences. The stories recorded here serve my recovery and as cautionary tales for other daring souls. Proceed with care into what follows. If you know any protective words, say them now.

Chapter One: 1850 - 1928

Family Exodus

This is my family story. It begins in the early 1850s even though I was not born until 1945. It ranges geographically from Jewish settlements in Poland and Russia to the mean streets of New York and Chicago where some tough Jews found themselves attracted to the early growth of organized crime.

Let me begin at the beginning. Freda Rachel Leah Wasserman, my great-great-grandmother, married a man named Yonah Hernreich, and was the mother of thirteen children. Like prophets of old, she saw the writing on the wall. Leaving her husband and children in Poland, she ventured across the Atlantic in 1850 to seek fortune for herself and her family in the United States. Family stories tell us that this remarkable woman returned to Poland five times to bring her entire family to the United States while liberating nearly $250,000 from Poland, averaging $50,000 of gold and jewels per trip, secreted in her luggage.

Through oft-repeated stories like this one, we learned that great-great-grandma had nightmares about Russian Cossacks killing all the Jews in Poland and Russia by fire. By 1903, as a result of her nightmares, she personally liberated each and every one of her children and their families from what she believed to be a potentially horrific threat. Ironically, her nightmares came true, just seven years after her death in 1932. It was, however, Nazi Germany and not Russia that perpetrated the Holocaust genocide in Europe.

Tough Jews

The story deepens and darkens a bit later in two distinct cities with closer ties than one might otherwise imagine. New York and Chicago, from the earliest part of the twentieth century through the late 1950s, were hubs for organized crime. While most people think exclusively of Italians at the head of organized crime, certain tough Jews in both New York and Chicago proved integral to the growth of gangster activity across the United States.

By 1914 in Chicago, for example, while Johnny Torrio ran the Italian Mob, my grandmother's two brothers, my Great-Uncles Ben and Felix Melnick were being described in the pre-WWI press as "well-known firebugs" after both brothers were arrested, convicted of arson with the intent to defraud, and sentenced to prison in Illinois. Interestingly, there is no record of either Ben or Felix being incarcerated for even one day and all evidence of their convictions seems to have strangely disappeared.

Ben, a lawyer and member of the Illinois Bar, likely had both convictions reversed and the records sealed, perhaps by forces of the Torrio organization. Ben continued to practice law in Chicago, representing gangsters for the Torrio organization, which was comprised not only of Italians, but also of Jews and Irish factions focusing on gambling, prostitution, and loan sharking.

In fact, by the early 1920s, Uncle Ben's law practice was thriving, a practice in which he represented the Capone family by 1923. His felony conviction notwithstanding, a conviction that should have barred him from practicing law, he was and remained a member of the Illinois Bar through the early 1930s, when he disappeared from Illinois only to resurface some 20 years later.

Uncle Felix, a motion picture projectionist, was one of the organizers of the projectionists' union in New York and Chicago, a powerful union controlled by the mob. Those gangster connections ran deeply through both sides of my family tree.

In New York, tough Jews like my paternal great-uncle, Harry Teitelbaum, along with Meyer Lansky, Joseph Rosen, Harry Greenburg, Louis Buckhalter and Arnold Rothstein became known as Murder, Inc., a group of assassins. Around the time of Prohibition, joined by Benjamin "Bugsy" Siegel and Lucky Luciano, the New York gangsters and their counterparts in Chicago added rum-running to their already profitable corrupt activities.

A contemporary of Ben Siegel, Alphonse Capone and his brother, Ralph, joined another brother, Frank, in Chicago. The Capone parents were already in Chicago when Al and Ralph joined Frank. Seeking to escape from New York's intense police activity, the three Capone brothers found themselves connected by mutual interests to the Torrio gang and to my Great Uncles, Ben and Felix. Ironically, the police threats they sought to escape were never as brutal as their own mobster activities.

Meanwhile, my father, Pop "Al" Teitelbaum, who was the great-nephew of Harry Teitelbaum and a boyhood friend of Ben Siegel, moved to Chicago around the same time as Al Capone. Two powerful New York and Chicago families were ultimately cemented when my father and mother married.

Merger of Perfectionism and Power

My grandparents, Tillie and Herman Melnick, were second cousins so when they married, Tillie's name did not change. Along with their first-born child, Perry, they joined Tillie's parents, Pesach Maier Melnick and Ida Hernreich Melnick, and Tillie's brothers, Ben and Felix, as the last of our family to leave the old country. Pesach and Ida were Russian-Polish Jews who were welcomed by Ida's mother, Frieda, to New York as she reassembled the whole family, down to fourth cousins and their extended families; lucky for us.

Because of its segregated neighborhoods, Great-Grandmother Ida was drawn away from New York City to Chicago's diverse and more intimate neighborhoods in which our family thrived for many years. Grandpa Herman crafted venetian blinds and served as a Cantor, singing prayers at the B'nai Zion, a Conservative synagogue in Chicago. He often told the story of how his gift of song served well when he was forcefully recruited into the Russian army. Instead of active duty, he was assigned to teach the Russian officers' wives how to sing. Such was the luck of this Melnick!

He also often told his ten children and all of his grandchildren how lucky we were to be living in America. Chicago offered a thriving Jewish community setting, but he emphasized how important it was to break with tradition in order to blend in with both Jews and gentiles who came before us. He was clear that if our family was going to survive in America, we had better act like Americans.

All of Herman's children were raised lighting candles on Friday night, a Jewish ritual to bring in the Sabbath. Our grandparents found it easier to migrate to the Conservative Jewish movement, not only because the synagogue was close to their home and business, but outside of the home it allowed their behavior to be as American as apple pie. In my immediate family, we celebrated traditional American holidays including Christmas. However, when praying, Grandfather still wore a Keppa (skull cap), Tallies (fringed prayer shawl), and Tifillin (two small ritual boxes worn on the head and one arm), and kept all the Jewish Holidays. His daily prayer rituals were elaborate and heart-warming to his loving family members.

My grandparents' ten children were born every two years, beginning in 1901 with the birth of Perry in Poland, in this order: Perry, Rose, Esther (Mom), Florence, Sara, Alvin, Chane, Hannah, Norma, and Rebecca. The two-year interim between births, according to many stories told by my mother and aunts, was attributed to Tillie's breast-feeding birth-control method. The sisters and brothers, my aunts and uncles and one parent, often liked to say if it is odd (referring to the year) you're even (referring to age.)

Much was made of how strong a mother Grandma Tillie was. She had to be strong to raise a brood of kids while constantly being pregnant. The devotion to "mama" by her children was strong and almost seemed dysfunctional. I never heard my mother or any of my aunts or uncles say a bad word about her. Even during their adult years, Tillie maintained strong matriarchal control over her children. Herman was never a match for Tillie when it came to family rule, deferring to her in every decision.

Mom was born in Chicago in 1905. As the third of ten children, Mom was expected to serve in a role much like that of a domestic servant, caring for six younger siblings. The Melnick children were both smart and independent and my mother was no exception. She attended Chicago Public Schools, the Stephen Haytt (pronounced Hate) Elementary School and went on to High School at Senn High. She also went to religious school at B'nai Zion where she learned the fundamentals of living a Jewish life.

It was clear that Mom was a natural in school. She worked hard and schoolwork came easy for her; her grades reflected a love of learning and she consistently showed up on the honor roll. Having to change a dirty diaper or to stir the soup on the stove often interrupted her studies, but none of that stopped her from dreaming big. She was a dutiful daughter who, like her siblings before her and those who came after, said "yes, mama" without question, at least in the early years, but without ever abandoning her dreams.

As she grew older, Mom began to think the unthinkable, that she could live an independent life as a professional woman, as a lawyer in a man's world and do more than just survive. In the fall of 1923, as she helped with preparations for breaking the Yom Kippur fast, Mom finally had enough. She ripped off her apron, grabbed her impressive high school transcript, marched out of the house, and headed straight into John Marshall Law School's Admissions Office; she was twenty years old by this time. It is clear that Mom's inclinations were not domestic and truly never would be.

Mom was one of the first females accepted into any law school. Not unexpectedly, her academic performance was exceptional, and she graduated from John Marshall Law School in 1927. In spite of her emotional outburst, Mom lived with her parents in their three-story wood home on Clark Street in Chicago both before and during her law school enrollment. In that context, someone might ask what any woman was doing in law school beginning in 1923. Mom was one of many in my family who, once they developed some personal strength, found social conventions more convenient to dissolve than not.

Only one year following my mother's birth, my father, Abraham Teitelbaum, was born in New York City, in the same Five-Corners Brooklyn neighborhood as his lifelong friend Benjamin Siegel, who was also born in 1906. He had other connections to tough Jews in New York as well. Another Jews who came of age during the prohibition era was Meyer Lansky.

In 1924, Pop moved away from New York City to attend John Marshall Law School in Chicago. He first boarded with Grand Uncle Abram Teitel since he wanted to live with family members. Abram's home was full to the brim with distant cousins, without even sufficient floor space for Pop to make a comfortable bed. His parents later sent him to live with family friends, Tillie and Herman Melnick. It is likely that this arrangement was brokered through Uncle Ben since he knew people in New York who were connected to the Teitelbaums.

The Clark Street house was the scene of wonderful chaos. Pop joined Tillie and Herman, eight daughters, two sons, and Tillie's brothers. While Uncle Ben and Uncle Felix did not know my father until he came to Chicago, they shared common interests and associates. It was during this period that Uncle Ben represented the Capone family, including Al Capone's mother and father.

Mom always claimed that Pop left New York and moved into the Melnick house in order to escape a forced arranged marriage in New York City. Mom was already in her second year of Law School when my father arrived; he asked and she successfully wrote and filed the papers to annul Pop's purportedly unconsummated marriage. The year was 1926 and Mom's research was, as always, detailed and perfect. Mom and Pop continued to work hand in hand throughout their education; today we might refer to them as study buddies but it was likely much more than that.

My father graduated from John Marshall Law School in 1928, already deeply in love with Mom who had become a fiercely independent and intelligent woman. Pop was 5'10" and 200 pounds, very good looking with dark brown eyes and a killer smile. Mom stood 5'4" tall, weighed 125 pounds, and was a beautiful woman with high cheekbones, large, corn silk blue eyes, and very dark brown curly hair. In spite of and perhaps in defiance of the moral standards of the twenties, Mom and Pop lived together as man and wife without a marriage ceremony for many years.

During her law school years, Mom took up boxing as a sport. She never tired of reminding us that she developed a good overhand right and was known in the amateur boxing world as "Kid Melnick". She loved to tell the story of the time when the captain of the Chicago State University football team looked down his nose at her and taunted her in a challenging tone. "Girls can't box," he snidely remarked. Pop immediately asked him to support his convictions with a $20.00 bet. Mom broke out the gloves and gave the six foot two football captain a severe, two-minute lesson in boxing, culminating with her notorious overhand right, which slapped the Captain flat on his backside. It was a humbling event, having been flattened by a petite woman with a mean overhand right.

In what could be the first of Pop's many gambling stories, he won the $20.00 bet and he took Mom out for a celebratory dinner at the Continental Plaza Hotel on North Michigan Avenue. Mom's skills were not limited to boxing; the full extent of her sparring talents would be revealed during a busy law career where her overhand right was, in practice, her attention to detail and rigorous research skills. Coupled with her cunning legal mind, she was capable of flattening nearly all of her opponents.

While both Mom and Pop scored quite high on intelligence scales, there were distinct and complimentary differences between them. Mom helped Pop with schoolwork because of her senior status and attention to detail. However, Pop's total recall gave him content mastery even after reading a book only once. He could take Mom's briefs and with the ease of a magician translate them into focused action. Mom, on the other hand, preferred working in the background focusing on her research where she left absolutely no stone unturned regarding the matter at hand. Her attentiveness to family matters was, however, much less focused; her distance and lack of focus negatively affected those who, by the mere accident of birth, came to be dependent upon her.

Chapter Two: 1928 - 1932

Digging for Debt

What seems clear is that Grandma Tillie was friendly with Al Capone's mother, Theresa. What is less clear, but open to delicious speculation, is how they became friends. Here is my best guess. When the Capone family came to Chicago and Al Capone became connected to the Torrio gang, my great uncles Ben and Felix Melnick were already connected to Johnny Torrio. Recall that Ben and Felix were convicted of 'arson for profit' in 1914, but there is no record of the two ever serving a day in prison. Once the Capone family arrived in Chicago around 1920, Ben Melnick represented Al Capone's parents and when Johnny Torrio 'retired' it is likely that Ben represented Al Capone himself in some matters as well. Ben probably introduced Theresa Capone to his sister Tillie. The two women became fast friends and just like sisters, they exchanged Italian and Jewish recipes.

Uncle Ben was a notorious gambler, often losing a great deal of money gambling on football, baseball, and ponies. The only way to explain these losses for a man as well connected as Uncle Ben is that he was addicted to the thrill of the bet and often failed to make good use of his connections. There are conflicting reports about whether Ben was an attorney or an accountant. Perhaps the line between the two was as blurred as many other boundaries in my family.

Just being employed by the Capones, however, was no protection from the collectors. Ben asked for Mom's assistance in the form of money to avoid the collectors' physical threats: broken feet, a broken arm, and missing teeth. In a classic 'enabling' relationship, Mom repeatedly paid off Ben's debts to bookies. Unfortunately, Uncle Ben never seemed to learn a lesson and his losses grew over the years. He was shocked when Mom eventually told him she would no longer pay his gambling debts. Finally, he hot-footed it to Canada, still owing $30,000.00 to the mob collectors, who were left holding the bag and therefore looked to Ben's family for restitution.

The obvious solution was for Tillie and Herman to sign their house over to the mob and settle Ben's $30,000 debt. Instead, Tillie came up with a plan and convinced Mom and Pop to offer the Capones their legal services as compensation for Ben's liability.

As a result, Mom and Pop's first long-term clients were Gabriel and Theresa Capone, Al's parents. Ben's gambling debt problem had been resolved while more than a lifetime of problems for the Teitelbaums had just begun. With this decision, Mom and Pop's relationship to the Capones was sealed and much of my life path was charted long before my birth.

Ben did not return from Canada until he made a brief appearance in 1950, when Grandma and Grandpa celebrated their 50th anniversary in Los Angeles. He didn't show up after that until 1964, when, still penniless and needing a place to live, Mom took him in until his death. His dying wish to be interred near his deceased wife in Chicago was fulfilled when his ashes were mailed to the cemetery via parcel post, book rate, in order to save on shipping fees.

Friend of the Family

By the crash of 1929, Mom and Pop were the darlings of Chicago. Under an annual retainer rate of $125,000 per client, their client list expanded from Gabriel and Theresa Capone to also include Ralph Capone, Al Capone, Benjamin Siegel, and Moses, the owner of Chicago's first sports wire. Their waiting list was growing rapidly.

With assistance from mob members, Pop was appointed Chief Council of "The Chicago Restaurant Union". This was an excellent position for him since hotel owners needed the Union's support to avoid strikes and ensure smooth business functions. Hotels and restaurants courted Pop's favor by frequently giving him complimentary services. In return for the assignment, Pop enforced hotel contracts with Union businesses such as laundry, food supplies, and other related services. In Chicago, the Unions provided the music and all of the management danced.

Mom, meanwhile, became the hero of the downtrodden and understood the severity of food scarcity among the populace. It was her personal conviction that she had a responsibility to provide food for the people of Chicago. In a show of support, Pop put pressure on their 'clients' to help organize soup kitchens. Mom and Pop funneled money from mobsters directly into food banks, hoping to improve the mobsters' public image while also serving their own personal mission.

These were definitely tough times for people living in the streets. The 'clients' were happy and gained public esteem for supporting unemployed community members who otherwise were unable to feed their families. It would be many years later in a different part of the country when Mom would understand more intimately what is was like to worry about feeding her own family and to depend upon others' goodwill.

Together, Mom and Pop were the "Great Chicago Mouthpieces," and served as the power that kept friends of mobsters out of Jail. They excelled in the art of making a deal. When there was going to be "blood in the streets" between warring Chicago factions, Pop could sit both sides down and broker a deal where neither side won or lost. These tactics kept the peace most of the time. However, sometimes things did not work out so well. Then condolence flowers were sent out and the problems just "went away". At a personal level, there were no obvious signs of conflict between Pop and Mom during this period.

The New Drake Hotel

In order to be closer to the office, Mom and Pop moved into the New Drake Hotel in 1929, only two years following its construction. It was easy and comfortable to live in this opulent apartment lifestyle; all a person needed was money. During their early years at the Drake, they traveled between home and office by either cab or limousine. Whether they went to the office together or separately, the use of public transportation was still easy and safe for them, at least for the moment.

Mom's sister, Hannah, started working as Mom and Pop's secretary when she was just seventeen. An intelligent and pretty young woman with a good sense of humor, Hannah was a trustworthy and loyal to my parents. She anticipated exactly what they needed in addition to attending to the routine office tasks like typing papers, fielding phone calls, and listening to horse races on the "wire".

Both Mom and Aunt Hannah often spoke of the many occasions when Hannah was caught pitching quarters with one of the firm's clients, Benjamin Siegel. Aunt Hannah said fondly, more times than I can count, "Ben was always a perfect gentleman and always dressed smart". It's not clear whether there were some romantic sparks between the two of them; no one ever spoke about it. What is true, however, is that she remained single until she eventually developed a long-term relationship with a man who served as our family's chauffeur, bodyguard, and personal tormentor, Carlos.

Hannah was not just a secretary in a mobbed-up law firm, not just one listening to the 'wire' or pitching quarters with Benjamin Siegel; she was a trusted courier as well. The late 20s and 30s era was low-tech, a time when money changed hands directly and not by wire transfer. During this time Mom and Pop often needed money for debt payments, bribes, or other under-the-table purposes.

For this they called on Mom's sister. Hannah, it seemed, always carried a "hatbox" while out in public. At any time the hatbox contained $25,000.00 or more as a ready source of cash for Pop's payoffs for or debt payments to clients within the city. Hannah carried the silver-bowed, black and white hatbox either by herself or in the company of some of her other sisters on Chicago's public transportation system: bus lines, the subway, or elevated trains. It was the family substitute for a bank, a handcuffed briefcase, or even a strongbox. Nobody ever caused problems or threatened Hannah when she transported large amounts of money in that unobtrusive hatbox.

Diamond Back

Most mobsters, like those in my family, needed to simply endure certain relatives who caused them trouble. Aunt Ilana, Pop's sister, was not at all fond of Mom. In cahoots with her mother, Ilana attempted to derail Mom and Pop's relationship by taking him to Europe on a long, slow, two-month cruise. There was always something unusual and edgy about Ilana and Pop's relationship, as though Ilana had a sense of entitlement to his life. The animosity between Ilana and Mom seemed stronger than sibling rivalry, with both of them vying for Pop's attention. The further Ilana could push Mom away from Pop, the more satisfied she seemed to be.

Unfortunately, my parental grandmother and aunt did not enjoy the company of my mother or any of the other Melnicks who spoke in high Yiddish without slang. Melnick conversations were pleasant to the ear. On the contrary, Teitelbaums used slang or low Yiddish with a guttural accent. The distinctions and biases were a sore point between our two families and created a chasm, which contributed to preventing the Melnicks and Teitelbaums from enjoying warm-hearted storytelling together.

In retrospect, it is hard to understand how either family looked down their nose at the other. They were both deeply intertwined with the Chicago outfit and the New York mob. My parents' marriage really helped to seal the corruptions among all involved.

Pop's family lineage also produced other professionals. His sister, Ilana, who was a smallish woman standing only about five feet tall, was also an attorney. She wore her wealth in the form of large diamond bracelets stacked up along her entire right and left forearms. She had been previously married to a Count, earning her the title, Countessa. Ilana had a mean streak through, which was apparently easily triggered by anything my mother said. The two of them were creative with their sometimes subtle but always relentless jabs. Just one example serves to illustrate the venomous nature of their feud. When Pop and Mom eventually married in 1932, Ilana sent Pop a telegram which read, "Did you have to get married to that woman?" implying that Mom was already pregnant.

It appeared as though these two tough old birds stayed alive just to taunt each other; Ilana lived until age 102 and Mom lived until age 90. There were plenty of opportunities for the two of them to share social time over the years, but they almost never had anything civil to say to one another. Their conversations were like verbal sparring, with Mom the more adept of the two. An overhand right might have been gentler in the long run.

Love Conquers All

Ultimately, with all family objections aside, Pop and Mom legalized their relationship. On July 19, 1932, The Herald Examiner said "Cupid Wins in Traffic Case".

> "Cupid came to the rescue of Abraham Teitelbaum Esq. and Esther Melnick Esq. today as they were arraigned in the Traffic Court for driving past a stop light.

> In their defense Mr. Teitelbaum told Judge Leon Edelman: "Well, your Honor, I did run through the stop light but in mitigation, I would say I was on my way to Crown Point, Indiana, with Miss Melnick. We are to be married." Judge Edelman freed them immediately. As a wedding present, the Judge gave them the green light and a police motorcycle escort to the state line where they were married, then they headed off to New York City for their honeymoon."

Mom and Pop were eventually forced to abandon public transportation and commute to work at the Fine Arts building, located at 410 South Michigan Avenue and previously known as the Studebaker building, by private driver in a limousine. Their office covered the entire 10th floor, including a large waiting room and an office suite as big as a house. Looking down from their office, visitors could see the beautiful Buckingham Fountain and a clear view of Lake Michigan.

In order to serve their confidential clientele, Pop built an extensive, legal library within their law office exclusively for Mom's use. It was quite a showpiece and word was that it exceeded University standards, but Mom was the only one allowed to use the library. She alone served all of Pop's needs for case review and research. His success was highly dependent upon her expertise.

A year after Mom and Pop were married, things were going very well at the office, and everything they wanted seemed to be within their reach. As was their habit, they dined with friends and clients nearly every evening. On one fateful evening the restaurant at which they were meeting with friends was only a short distance from their office. They decided to walk the six blocks to join their friends, even though it was cold and a little lake snow had already fallen. Everyone seated at the table that evening enjoyed a fine dinner; they dined and socialized until just before midnight.

With hats and coats in hand, Abraham and Esther walked out through the restaurant's double doors into a light snow. It was very cold and they asked the doorman to get them a "Yellow Cab", who advertised on their doors that they would deliver customers safely to their destination. The fleet of Chicago's Yellow Cabs was very popular, particular when weather was difficult.

While driving home, their cab driver plowed into another car as it ran a red light. Mom was rushed to the hospital by ambulance with a severely damaged neck. At first the doctors said she broke her neck. She was immobilized in the hospital for a couple of months and continued to need traction therapy for many years thereafter.

Of course, Mom engaged in legal research during her convalescence and Pop filed a suit against the yellow cab company. The cab company soon withdrew the word 'safe' from their advertising as a result. Ever since the accident, Mom always walked stiffly, as if she had a coat hanger sewn into the neck and shoulders of her jacket.

Building the Empire

The Teitelbaum Empire was growing still growing when Pop acquired ownership of The Chicago Fine Arts Building, 30 North LaSalle, as well as four other major downtown properties. Pop never mortgaged anything; instead he secured free and clear ownership of multiple properties; it was, after all, the 1930s and the Great Depression caused the value of real estate to plummet down to all-time lows. Pop was acting as an optimistic investor, realizing that the market could only go up. Plentiful cash assets were exchanged for these transactions, either in lawyer's briefcases, hatboxes, or large manila envelopes. Perhaps Pop served as a surrogate landowner for his gangster clients but it was his name that appeared on the real estate title, so who is really to say?

There was also a growing concern for Pop's personal safety arising from his deep involvement in gangster activity as the years unfolded. Not all gangsters, however, wanted to harm Pop. He specialized in making deals and could talk to Union leaders in their own language. He knew the squeaky wheels and was not reluctant to apply grease. Pop could arrange a sit-down with the best of the worst. As a Labor Relations Attorney, he was gifted in making his associates happy during these years. That gift was clearly lost on his emerging family, though, every one of whom he eventually abandoned to life's ill fates.

Chapter Three: 1938 – 1946

A New Prince and a Deal You Can't Refuse

Albert, the new family prince, was born December 15, 1938. His birth and the lives of all siblings who followed him are owed to Pop's negotiating skills; Mom was not at all interested in being fruitful and multiplying. Pop, on the other hand, believed that it was important for children to carry on his successful legacy and share the family's expansive new wealth. It was difficult for Mom to reconcile her professional passions with family life responsibilities, but she eventually succumbed to Pop's undeniable charms.

It must have been especially difficult for Mom when Albert's severe colic and continuous crying led managers of the Drake to evict Mom and Pop. Fortunately, when one of their clients reportedly needed money in 1938, the client's house on 538 Hawthorn Place became conveniently available. Mom and Pop "bought" it and moved in with the new baby; a deal they couldn't refuse.

A leather-bound inventory still exists showing that the house was "sold" with all of its furnishings, from a double Steinway piano valued at $120.00 to all of the previous owners' personal clothing, linens, and silverware. Although the house and its contents were valued at a total of $80,000.00, the Teitelbaums purchased the entire package for a mere $20,000.00. It causes one to wonder and perhaps even shiver at the thought of the arm-twisting and the broken bones that likely occurred in order for this house to be so readily and conveniently available for my parents. The Hawthorne Place house was just what Pop needed to start his dynasty.

With big brown eyes like Pop, dark hair, and a great smile, Albert was brought up as a favored child. The entire family, including my mother's sisters and brothers, doted on his every sound, need, and action. He was showered with attention from governesses, doctors, and family members. As the first-born boy, he was entitled to a privileged life in a very important family. The way Prince Albert was cared for reminded me of how European royalty is treated in all of its glory and grandeur.

Extra, Extra!

Pop was never bothered by the idea of mixing business with family. In fact, business came first for both my parents but Pop was just more open about his role. He loved to tell the story about a chance meeting with one of his childhood friends. Pop told the tale about how one day, while he was standing on a street corner in Chicago, Jackson and Michigan, he reached into his pocket to make sure his wallet was still there and found, to his surprise, that he was shaking hands with his old friend Benjamin Siegel.

Pop and Benjamin Siegel knew each other from their boyhood days in Brooklyn. Both were born in 1906 and lived in the same Brooklyn neighborhood, a neighborhood that apparently produced a bunch of "tough Jews". There is a reason to believe that the two not only knew each other but also came to maturity under many of the same influences. If this is true, and I have no reason to doubt it, then much of Pop's business follows from the circumstances of his birth. In addition, Benjamin Siegel was an acquaintance of Harry Teitelbaum, Pop's uncle, and they were likely involved in rum running with Meyer Lansky.

Pop told me that Benjamin Siegel was always doing deals in Hollywood, which usually involved Unions and, of course, Unions were Pop's specialty. Benjamin and his thugs first controlled the Teamsters' Union and later the Screen Extras Guild (SEG) during the filming of Gone With the Wind. The SEG was especially useful when friends from Chicago were "too hot to work", which is gangster language for "being on the lamb" or "hiding from the law". Those Chicago friends could easily find work in Hollywood as extras. The money was not good but they all had their own scams going on the side to bring in cash. The SEG gave them a place to network in safety.

Bookies, mobsters, hoods, and whores could always play their own characters in Hollywood. Their look was great, they had all the right clothing, and they could "hide in plain sight" by working for the studios.

Living Large

Even though it was the basis of their personal and professional associations, the mobster subculture took quite a toll on my parents' marriage relationship. Mom was regularly upset with Ralph Capone who picked up Pop once or twice a week for "business meetings" at night. Instead, they went to parties at houses of ill repute run by Sheeny Rose Moses, a local madam of some reputation, and others. Pop did not drink much or smoke, but he relished the sleazier side of life, hanging with gangsters, bookies, and 'loose' women.

When he came home with no booze on his breath, his suit perfect, and a smile on his face, Mom knew that Pop's clothing had been hanging in a closet while he was in bed with a couple of women from the shady side of town. This was a continuing problem, which followed him throughout the remainder of his life.

Pop often stayed away from home for a few days at a time. As a labor relations attorney, he told Mom that he had Restaurant Union business, but Mom knew the truth. He was holding court as the big player. By this time he weighed over 300 pounds and sweated his way through court.

Mom managed to stay busy pulling research from the library, offering a reprieve from Pop's demanding company of characters who were playing craps, throwing quarters, and taking up space in both the law office and their home on Hawthorne Place.   Providing relief from her anger and disappointment, Pop's absences always opened up welcome time for Mom to work on legal cases without distractions. If she had concerns about her husband's whereabouts, none of us heard those objections or any acrimony at all between the two of them. In fact, upon his return, Pop was rewarded with beautifully crafted legal research, which made him look like a hero as he delivered Mom's articulate legal justifications in court.

Nobody would ever have accused my father of doing anything small. He always said if he was in for a penny, he was in for a dollar. Pop's total recall made it easy for him to read and remember anything from complex legal briefs to the racing forms. Therefore, he was very successful at gambling for many years, even when the race wasn't fixed. He was the attorney for the first wire service in Chicago, a synchronous telephone reporting service for racing results, so he also received early tips about successful races. The information allowed him to "beat the odds;" then the payoff allowed him to spread his impressive wad of cash around to friends, gangsters, women, and bookies.

He typically kept a ten thousand dollar roll of bills wrapped with a fat rubber band in one pocket and a set of business cards likewise wrapped in the other. Pop had two character traits that served him well throughout his life. He was a gifted chameleon and he was a strategic thinker. He verbally mirrored the company he was in, whether it was a mobster, client, judge, or merely a friend. In a way, he was mirroring their style of speech and idiosyncratic language while presenting himself as a sympathetic soul. By so doing, he calculatingly endeared himself to others.

When I had a problem, Pop often pragmatically counseled me by saying he could eat an elephant one forkful at a time. That was the way he approached any problem, with conviction, attention to detail, almost inhuman endurance and straightforward pragmatism. The council he gave me was heartfelt, representing his solution directed approach to life in the midst of complex problems.

It was true that Pop lived large. At home he tried to play the role of a perfect husband and father. Away from home, however, he was transformed into a gambler and womanizer. On the one hand, he acted like a model family man; brought presents to the kids, put food on the table and feigned compliance with religious rituals, but his passions pushed him directly into hedonism. Moral values seemed to completely elude him.

Over the years Pop never looked back on anything or anyone. Once a decision was made, he wiped his hands clean of it, often gesturing as such by clapping and swiping his hands dramatically across each other. He expressed admiration for murderers and mobsters like Al Capone. One of his frequent references to Capone was, "He is the most honorable man I ever met. If he said he was going to kill you, he would."

Pop was typically polite and witty. He was never drunk, didn't smoke, and didn't do drugs; he was well known as a man who could "polish more brass by accident then ten men on purpose." People often said he was one of the most charming men they had ever met. Since he had a way with words, it was easy for him to get whatever he wanted through persuasion or by charming others through his ability to create limericks on the spot. He was able to set others at ease no matter what the circumstances. He strongly believed that attorneys with the best use of the English language were the ones who would generally win, because they could more easily sway the judge or a jury.

Blue-Eyed Girl Child

Celeste was born on February 10, 1942, and joined the family at Hawthorn Place. Gifted with Mom's blue eyes, Celeste was a very happy baby from the start. She had curly brown hair and a sweet nature, garnering a great deal of attention from family and servants. By the time she was about three, Albert often was asked to play with her. Even though he was three years older than Celeste, she quickly caught up with his pace and they developed what appeared to be a close relationship. However, the sad truth was that he delighted in tormenting Celeste by frightening her, threatening to suffocate her, locking her in the attic, pushing her down the stairs, and making her life generally miserable. In spite of the abundance of relatives around, Albert seemed to always find ways to torment her.

Some family members needed a place to stay after being discharged from World War II duties, and the house on Hawthorne was big enough to accommodate them. Others needed financial support for starting a business. Times were hard, family members were returning from the war, and Mom and Pop were reliable and respected family providers. In most families, these kindnesses would be repaid if the tables were ever turned. Reciprocation was not in the cards, however, at least for Mom. When fortune turned its back on her, family support was lean indeed.

A Real Firecracker

Eighteen months after Celeste's birth, Mom was pregnant again. She went into labor on the 4th of July, 1943, at 3:30 PM. The streets around Hawthorn Place and Lakeshore Drive were crowded because of the holiday celebrations, so Pop was forced to call an ambulance. Even the ambulance could not get through the crowded streets, so Pop then called upon his contacts at the local Police Station. Up the sidewalks came a classic police transport vehicle, the type used to haul away prisoners. Police officers loaded Mom and Pop into the back along with their private nurse. Anne Ruth Teitelbaum was born in the back of that vehicle on the way to Michael Reese Hospital, with sirens blazing and motorcycle escorts who opened a path in the crowd. Anne was born on the Fourth of July; to this very day she remains a real firecracker.

Anne was welcomed into the family and began walking early. By 14 months she was in step with Albert and Celeste and just slightly ahead of the harried governess. Ann also received loving attention from Aunt Hannah, who home-schooled all of us in reading, writing, arithmetic, singing, poetry, and dancing. In her early thirties now, Hannah's creative maternal instincts and intelligence were otherwise untapped. Through Hannah's tutelage, Anne's love of art was well established. She found her own creative niche, which became an enduring outlet throughout her life.

An unfortunate accident fueled a fire, which contributed to my family's alienation. Albert was about six years old when a Governess spilled boiling hot tea on him, severely scalding approximately 25% of the skin on the left side of his chest over his heart. The wound did not heal well in the tough Chicago winter, and the summer humidity was likewise not helpful. A family doctor insisted that Albert must be moved to a warmer climate for his health. Pop had many clients in Palm Springs, California; they encouraged him to move out West to better serve their own needs. That decision would be made in a short time.

Dousing the Chicago Fires

One afternoon, neighbors placed an alarming phone call to report their great concern upon seeing small children on the Hawthorne Place house's second-story roof. At ages five and six, Albert and cousin Henry climbed upstairs to one of the top floor windows, crawled outside and onto the roof. They walked without fear to the roof's edge. Pretending to put out the Great Chicago Fire, they pee'd off the roof into the well-manicured flower garden. After a severe scolding, both boys were warmly hugged, and released to continue running all over the house as was their custom.

During those hot Chicago summers, the maids filled galvanized steel washtubs with cool water for the young children to play in as a safer alternative to the indoor swimming pool. Albert, Celeste, and Anne splashed in the water-filled tubs to beat the heat and humidity. All of the children, including visiting cousins, had hours of fun splashing water onto the lawn while maids in starched white uniforms held vigil, armed with clean towels and refreshing drinks. At the end of playtime, not much water remained in the metal washtubs.

Initiated Into the Tribe

I was born on September 22, 1945, at Michael Reese Hospital, just 20 minutes before midnight. Named Robert John Teitelbaum, my eyes were the same color as my father's and my hair was light brown. The house was well staffed for childcare and I was easily integrated into the family routines. Albert was 7 years old the year I was born, still suffering from the scald burns; Celeste was 4; and Anne was just 2 years old. I learned to crawl by the age of 8 months, motivated by the desire to keep up with my busy siblings.

Al Capone sent a birth gift delivered to me by my father: child-sized cuff links fashioned from 14K gold; they were replicas of mother of pearl-handled .38 revolvers complete with rotating cylinders. I was 17 years old when I finally realized how profoundly inappropriate the cuff links were as gifts to celebrate a child's birth. Instead, they were sobering images of my early initiation into a cold, heartless, and complex brotherhood. The initiation, however minimal, was effective enough to eventually trigger my use of a .38 revolver before I turned fifteen.

Right around the time I was born, things were getting a bit unsettled around our house. Given the occupational hazards of representing gangsters, there were times that seemed more dangerous than others. From late 1943 to the time of my own birth, things were more or less unsettled for both Mom and Pop, raising concerns about family safety; their solution was "Nicky," a beautiful female Doberman Pincer who was intended to protect all of the Teitelbaum children from harm, real or imagined. She had undergone at least 6 months of training prior to arriving at our house. She was always called, "The Guard Dog."

Nicky played with me, my brother, and sisters in a very sweet way, never rough but always restrained. If someone new approached, however, Nicky stood at point in between the stranger and us. As a guard dog, she was a ferocious family protector. I always felt safe when she was nearby, even in the early years when I didn't know exactly what fear was. Somewhere deep inside, I sensed over the years that dark clouds of danger hovered, but at the same time I had no clue about whether that danger emanated from family, friend, or foe.

Nicky's size, bared long white teeth, and her general aggressive demeanor were intimidating to others. She was as black as a crow in a coalmine with a rich brown chest and muzzle. Nicky was never more than three feet away from me. Even in Chicago she saved my life, pulling me out of the indoor swimming pool when I was in danger of drowning. My Pop loved to tell me this story. To my later embarrassment, he also told my second grade class that same story during one of his visits to the schoolhouse. Pop was a frequent drop-in visitor at the school, and loved to throw his weight around. He felt that his congeniality would be endearing to the community. The closeness Nicky and I shared was constant. Despite my father's bravado, I believe that Nicky really did save my life.

My first memories of Mom, Pop, and the family go back to before I could walk or talk, although it is difficult to know which memories are distinct and which developed with the help of family storytelling through the years. Even though I remember many people caring for me, my mother's voice and embrace were distinctive and soothing. It seemed like Pop was around about as much as Mom, but not very much because they both worked long hours. It has always been said that I learned to swim long before I walked, perhaps because I was under the supervision of a governess and servants rather than the protection of self-absorbed parents. At six months, I was splashing in the large galvanized steel tubs placed outside on the lawn along with the rest of the children.

The house was filled with wonderful sensory experiences, from extraordinary meals to beautiful music. Every Wednesday and Thursday evening, the third floor music room came alive. String musicians from the Chicago Symphony graced our presence by rehearsing in the marble floored music room, accompanied by someone on the double Steinway piano. The excellent acoustics kept musicians coming back for more and we were their happy beneficiaries. For the Teitelbaum children, life was full, rich, and very happy during these years.

Wishing on a Star

Over the holidays at Hawthorn Place my aunts often brought their friends to visit. One Christmas in 1945, two of my aunts brought a young friend named Roxanne to share the holiday with us. Several family members were gathered together in a parlor, each one imagining aloud what they wanted in life. When asked what she would wish for, Roxanne looked into the living room, gestured toward the Norman Rockwell scene where Mom and Pop were hosting family members and friends, and then responded by stating assertively, "I want this". There is some evidence that Norma delighted in undermining Mom's marriage. Mom's hospitable nature and trust in her own family would have prevented her from suspecting that her own sisters could introduce a threat to her marriage. Roxanne was as welcome as any other visitor or family member.

Roxanne was only 17 years old when most of our family moved to Palm Springs, and it was approximately one year later when Roxanne's wish came true. She moved into our house with my father who was then 40 years old and that is when Pop started his second family. In practice, Pop lived a polygamous life for thirty-three years until Roxanne committed suicide just prior to her fiftieth birthday.

Chapter Four: 1947

Hello, Sunshine!

In late 1946 my family was uprooted from the luxury of our home on Hawthorne Place and moved abruptly to Palm Springs. The move was justified with a two-fold explanation: to help Albert recover from his slow-healing burn and as a means of protecting the family from the dangers in Chicago. The real reason that was never spoken out loud, as I came to learn, was to segregate Pop's two families from each other; creating space for both while keeping them isolated from one another. During this transition he was under attack from Union thugs who wanted his power to control the Chicago restaurant Union, so tensions ran high.

While Pop's first family made a new home in Palm Springs, he stayed in Chicago with Roxanne and his growing addictions to gambling, women, money, and gangsters. However, he visited us once or twice each year for many years. Those visits reinforced our relationship in some ways and tore us further apart in others. Mom and Pop began openly arguing about money and Pop's painfully obvious improprieties.

My siblings and I were uncomfortable with these arguments partly because we knew exactly how the bickering would end. Pop would leave us even sooner, ahead of schedule. Our precious, long-anticipated two weeks with him was quickly reduced to five or six days at best. Sometimes the visits were clearly intended to be a reprieve for Pop, as he sought respite from his younger family. He appeared to be exhausted when he arrived on our doorstep.

Aunt Hannah was one of the six family members leaving from Chicago's Midway airport in 1946 for the long trip to Palm Springs. I was 10 months old at the time. While Hannah shepherded Albert, Celeste, and Anne to the airplane, Mother prepared to pick up and carry me. My first walking steps were taken at that moment, in the airport. The airplane noise was very difficult for me on this long trip. To the consternation of all, I put up quite a fuss and required a great deal of attention from Celeste and Anne, who tried to entertain me. At age 8, Albert was already a busy boy, exploring as much of the airplane as possible. Nicky was crated and carried in the airplane's luggage compartment for the trip across country.

When we arrived at the Palm Springs airport, two big limousines were waiting to pick us up. We were delivered in style to our new homes, two adjacent houses located on Tamarisk Street.

A flock of staff members, hired in advance, met us at the front door. There was a driver, a cook, an English butler, a governess, and two maids, all of whom were smartly dressed, perfectly pressed, and seasonally appropriate. Each house had between 5 and 7 bedrooms and the neighborhood was buzzing with questions about a family who needed two houses. The Teitelbaums had arrived! This was big news in a small town; our background was associated with enough question marks to fuel the rumor mills.

During the hot summer months, I loved placing my face on the playroom's cool black and white marble floor and nearby I had a large bedroom next to my sisters, Celeste and Anne. Albert had a room upstairs. Celeste and Anne remember playing a game of catch with me as I tossed glass baby bottles to them. They could catch them most of the time.

My favorite place in our house was a rocking chair with a pillow. When I rocked, the attached music box entertained me. I loved our new home and felt secure with Nicky nearby. She was always right by my side and it also seemed as though both of the houses were constantly filled with attentive relatives. The Tamarisk houses offered us a short-lived safe haven.

America tested an early atomic bomb at Bikini Island in 1946. While living on Tamarisk, Albert and Celeste began 'duck and cover' bomb drills in a Palm Springs school. They dropped to the floor under their desks, covered the back of their heads and necks with fingers laced together, kept their knees and elbows on the floor, and waited for the loud high pitched school siren to run its course. When the sirens stopped, everyone knew that the atomic mushroom threat had passed and life then went on as usual. The Teitelbaum family's threats, however, were not yet on our horizon; no amount of drills could have protected us from the upcoming internal hazards. Home life was still exciting, rich, and full.

As it turned out, the two Tamarisk houses were actually too small for all of our 50 plus relatives who came to stay for three to four weeks during the summers. We sold the Palm Springs houses to Pop's brother, Uncle Michael, at a large discount and held the mortgage paper for him. It is not clear why Michael was encouraged to take advantage of this excellent offer, an offer that would have been be hard to refuse. Michael had six children.

The Loveless Estate

There were two properties built in the Coachella Valley by Walter Kirschner, a larger than life character who always wore a white ten-gallon hat. One of his properties was the Old Tower Ranch in La Quinta, and the second facility, the Loveless Ranch, was built as a private retreat for President Roosevelt's retirement years. When the Ranch was built in 1943, wood was rationed. If not for government intervention, building materials would not have been available. In this case, though, wood was delivered from Los Angeles under the cover of darkness.

Roosevelt unfortunately died before he could enjoy the 'Shangri-La' resort intended for his comfort. Some might see this misfortune predicted in the property's original name, Loveless Ranch, which continued to visit misfortune on other inhabitants. The origin of the name, Loveless, is unclear but nonetheless significant and highly predictive.

Eleanor Roosevelt and two of her adult children lived there in the summer of 1945. Her seasonal timing could not have been worse. She did not mince words in her evaluation of the climate, "It is too damn hot!" She packed up the family and returned home to Val Kill, New York, after only a couple of months living in the blistering Indio summer heat.

The Loveless Estate was then sold to Mom and Pop. Walter Kirschner was well respected in the Coachella Valley because of his land dealings, deep pockets, and support for important community projects. He knew Pop very well from Chicago and understood his need for a secure turnkey property. He sold the Loveless Ranch to my father for $129,000.00, fully furnished.

I was two and one-half years old when we were driven from Palm Springs to Indio in a big black limousine along with Nicky and the rest of the family. Mom was holding me on her lap, and Aunt Hannah was watching over Albert, Celeste, and Anne. As soon as the Loveless Ranch tour began, we were all wide eyed.

The ranch consisted of ten acres including a three acre internal compound enclosed by an eleven foot high, two to three foot thick, cement wall, painted snowy white and capped on top with large red bricks. The bricks were wide enough for small children to run along, sometimes flawlessly and other times dangerously. Immaculate rose gardens served as the catchment basin for falling children! More than once my skin was ripped open by rose thorns waiting to catch my fall. Since the sandy ground in the gardens was always well tended, it was soft enough to land on without causing more than thorny damage.

A five-room security house stood at the compound's entrance, built for Roosevelt's Secret Service employees. Although not within the three-acre compound, this area was separately enclosed by a tall snow-white wooden fence and a dramatic eighteen-foot, olive-green gate. Topping the gate was a heavy crossbeam from which hung a loud bell whose high-pitched tone could be heard across a great distance. It took four muscular men to hang that bell from the crossbeam. The bell was sometimes rung by visitors to request entry from the compound's bodyguards, and it was also used to call ranch hands for dinner, which I suppose was the real reason the bell was there in the first place.

Approximately forty cars could park inside the wooden fence next to the garages, chauffeurs' quarters, maids' quarters, and an outside equipment storage area. Near the maids' quarters was a secret or 'safe' hideout room, occupied by Benjamin Siegel during one of his many ranch visits.

An unobtrusive green gate led visitors from the security house area into the three acre protected compound, past a massive red brick barbeque with a chimney, which shadowed even the eleven-foot wall. Measuring approximately twelve feet long, an entire cow could be marched into the oven. Barbeques were frequent events, serving from twenty to more than one hundred guests.

We walked together through the immaculate gardens and into the house. The front door to the main house opened into a sixty-six by forty foot living room with two fireplaces on either side of the room, a huge formal dining table for twenty people, and elaborate furniture. There were six double floor-to-ceiling windows from which light flooded across the front of the house. On one side of the living room was a full bar which could easily accommodate thirty people, and included a large elaborate mirror with the initials, FDR, etched in scrolled lettering. The Loveless Ranch was built to entertain over 50 people for up to a month at a time.

The kitchen could easily feed one hundred people, with three massive stoves and four double-door refrigerators and a walk-in cooler for vegetables. A black and white marble island, eight feet long, four feet wide, and two inches thick, rested on a bank of cupboards. The marble's quality was not harmed by deep, daily cleansing. In some ways, the island was the center of activity and interest. I perfected Grandmother's potato latke recipe while working at this marble centerpiece over the years.

Every other day the milk truck arrived with fresh cold milk, butter, cheese, eggs, cottage cheese, sour cream, and Yami yogurt for Mom. One of the four refrigerators was reserved for milk alone. In addition there was a walk-in refrigerator specifically used for fresh produce. The driver was dressed in a crispy white uniform including a white cap with a black band and a black belt. He worked for about an hour, rotating dairy products in the refrigerators; on his way out he left a daily bill for our butler, who turned it over to Aunt Hannah for payment. As the hub of activity, food wasn't the only thing that turned over in the kitchen. Years following our arrival, Aunt Hannah and I both suffered dearly in this room at the hands of our abuser.

The thickly carpeted master bedroom had a large marble fireplace and two enormous beds with silk upholstered headboards. Lambskin rugs were scattered throughout the bedroom and the bathroom. Bedroom walls were darkly stained hardwood from floor to ceiling, requiring periodic oil treatments from the servants. Large window seating areas offered views from the lawns to the pool house.

The marble floored master bathroom's walls were purple tiled from floor to ceiling and the bathroom included a three-step down bathtub with sturdy handrails for Roosevelt's benefit. Four forty-gallon water heaters were required to fill the tub. An adjacent sit-down shower, enclosed on 3 sides, was tiled with the same blue and purple tiles as the tub. A large round ottoman style, white linen, sitting couch with a tall center was the bathroom's centerpiece. Every seat around the couch offered a comfortable backrest because of the elevated center.

Mom's law library had already been transferred to the ranch. It was accessed through a grand entryway from the master bedroom as well as a separate door from the bathroom. The entire library of books from Chicago found residence here, including Mom's licenses to practice law in front of the United States' Supreme Court. An avid reader, Mom's private reading collection was housed here, including works from the great masters. It was in this library that Mom continued to serve as a hero to downtrodden by tutoring some of our uneducated employees. It was also the site of numerous mother-child lectures about proper manners, gentlemanly and ladylike behavior. Errant children were required to sit in a chair crafted together from about twenty longhorn cow horns, covered by soft dark leather. The children were made to endure endless lectures from an articulate lawyer who would have done us a favor by substituting the lecture with an over-hand right.

We continued outside, around the Olympic swimming pool and into the rose gardens. The roses, date palms, citrus trees, and well-manicured lawns caused even my mother to break her calm demeanor with gasps of appreciation. It seems that Pop bought the ranch without any input from Mom; this was her first time seeing the whole thing.

Behind the house were beautifully tended date groves, grapefruit trees, blood orange trees, and a professional sized tennis court, all protected by a tall white wooden fence. Star jasmine plants were plentiful and when they were in bloom it would have been easy to mistake the ranch for heaven itself because of the exquisite aroma. Outside the kitchen was a separate fenced dog compound. In all, there were 4 fenced-in areas: the front of the house with chauffer's quarters, the main compound with the swimming pool and the big house, the dog compound, and the back yard. Fences can be deceiving. They can protect inhabitants from outside forces, prevent inhabitants from escaping abuse, or even prevent advocates from intervening on internal abuses.

Mom contracted to change the swamp-style water air conditioning to a full 5-ton refrigeration unit that kept the entire house cold. Gas was inexpensive at only 17 cents per gallon but the cost of electricity ran up to $400 per month. Cooling one of the largest houses in the Coachella Valley did not come cheap.

An ever-flowing water well was capped even before we arrived. When I was about 6 years old I was given the daily chore to uncap the well, fill up the cistern, and open a 4-foot wide concrete pipe to let the water flow into the date grove for irrigation. Thirty seconds after uncapping the well, the water was ice cold. I would brace myself, lean my face into the flowing water, and drink until it felt like my stomach would burst. Even though it was the best tasting water ever, it usually gave me brain freeze. This is one of my fondest memories from the Loveless Ranch. After watering the grove, I still had to fill the 10,000-gallon water tanks daily for the swimming pool, refrigeration, and gardens. The task usually took approximately one-half hour.

A beautiful Olympic size swimming pool was within the three acre fenced compound, and a 1,500 square foot changing room was nearby. It included gender specific restrooms, lockers, two fireplaces, well-appointed furniture, and evaporative cooling.

As soon as we arrived, a few shopkeepers with whom we had business let us in on local gossips' stories, claiming that Mom was Al Capone's sister; such stories were sources of laughter for all of us. That rumor was also printed in a local publication about the Loveless Ranch history.

Nicky Knew Best

Nearing the end of the Loveless Ranch tour, Mom was carrying me in the north side yard when twenty-year-old Carlos Martén, who approached us dressed in a black suit and cap, suddenly interrupted us. As he moved forward to introduce himself, Nicky growled loudly. Carlos paused only briefly, advanced again, and extended his hand, which prompted Nicky to charge him. Nicky chased Carlos, screaming and yelling, toward a palm tree surrounded at the base by a circular picnic table and a set of matching benches. Carlos jumped first onto a bench, then leaped onto the table and finally reached the palm tree fronds where he climbed further upward to safety from Nicky's snapping teeth. Carlos was certainly very fast, but Nicky did a great job of treeing him. Mom called Nicky off and she immediately stood down, but Nicky was right after all. She smelled evil and to this day I believe she would have preferred to taste it!

Fox in the Henhouse

Carlos Martén was a semi-pro boxer who worked for Walter Kirchner. At just twenty-years-old, he served as a bodyguard and carried a gun for Kirchner. Carlos was of Mestizo Indian descent with light brown skin, about 5' 4" tall, and weighing 150 pounds. He had a full head of wavy black hair and sinister dark eyes. When Walter was asked to build the estate house and compound, Carlos had already been working on the property. He grew up working in the ranch fields, had no formal education, and his large family knew hard times.

Carlos learned boxing at an early age and excelled at the sport as the years unfolded. He fought as an amateur in local clubs and the county fair. By sixteen years of age, Carlos earned a semi-professional title and helped support his family with cash prizes.

When not fighting, Carlos worked for Walter Kirchner, as his bodyguard under the title of Loveless Ranch foreman. Carlos was a tough guy with no apparent boundaries; he used his brutal anger to control others. As a graphic example, none of the ranch hands would challenge his orders without taking a beating and being sent on their way, tail between their legs. Carlos' unfettered anger and violent streaks were well known amongst friends and family.

As Kirchner's bodyguard, Carlos dressed in a smart black suit with cap and gun. He was working in this capacity when Eleanor Roosevelt and two of her adult sons were in residence. Along with the Secret Service, Carlos served as a community liaison and driver for the ranch. However, Secret Service personnel took Carlos' gun away before the Roosevelt party arrived. Perhaps they saw through the black suit and chauffeur's cap façade.

The first lady and her family members eventually left the oppressive summertime heat, and Carlos' gun was returned to him. Secret Service personnel who befriended Carlos also gave him a .38 Smith and Wesson revolver along with shooting lessons out in the date palm groves.

Walter then sold the furnished property to Pop, and Carlos was a clear choice to serve as the family bodyguard and chauffeur. Pop did not hesitate to offer Carlos $600 per month for his services, a fortune in 1947. Before accepting, Carlos consulted with Kirchner who agreed to let Carlos go. Carlos stayed on as ranch foreman, which included a nice residence on the property. It was Carlos' responsibility to protect our entire family when Pop was in Chicago or Florida. He was also responsible for running the ranch because of his earlier strong performance in that role.

Educating Carlos Martén

Mom believed that the privileged had a responsibility to help the less fortunate. While living in Chicago in 1929 to 1930, Mom researched, wrote, and argued the "Chicago Land and Trust Case," which stated that a person's home or property could not be taken away without due process. This was one of Mom's basic beliefs. Upon reflection, it's still a mystery how that philosophy squared with the Teitelbaum's $20,000 Chicago mansion 'bargain'.

Regardless, it troubled Mom that Carlos Martén only had a very basic education, which ended in fourth grade so he could work in the fields. By the time he was 15 years old, he had 20 brothers and sisters. Mom took it upon herself to educate Carlos, investing years in his education.

Starting in 1947, Mom taught Carlos how to read and write, then how to speak correct English, drawing from her complex law vocabulary. Mom opened her sacred library to Carlos and mentored him in legal banter. Carlos was an intelligent man, so the lessons came easy. A bond was created between Carlos and Mom during those years, a bond which promised to survive past all natural boundaries of motherly instincts and human reason, at a cost to every one of her children.

By the end of 1947, Carlos' vocabulary and grammar had improved dramatically. When addressed disrespectfully on the streets, he responded curtly, "I am not an illiterate Mexican farm worker," and chastised his critics roundly. The articulate rebukes he delivered could have come from an English professor, leaving his foes surprised and humbled in a challenging wake of verbal confrontation and abuse.

Carlos' intelligence included musical ability. He played classical guitar without squeaking the strings; his technique was flawless. He loved Mexican revolutionary songs from the 1913 to 1919 era. His musical performances were perfect. One of his uncles was a general in the revolutionary army, serving with Pancho Villa and other Mexican Generals. Carlos saw himself as a warlord and was constantly on alert for revolutionary opportunities. The words pillage and rape fit his personality style perfectly, just like a hand in a glove. It didn't take long at all before we became his victims as well. My innocent sisters were his first prey, at least the first in my immediate family to fall into his interminable lair.

Security Breach

Both Celeste and Anne remember Carlos as a mean, scary, and abusive man from the very beginning. Celeste described how he initiated her into sexual encounters when she was only 5 years old by requiring that she provide him with graphic "peeping Tom" opportunities. He threatened to get her into trouble if she refused.

Later, when he found out that Albert had already sexually abused Anne and Celeste, Carlos' abusive behaviors escalated. He forced both girls individually to reveal and demonstrate details of Albert's incestuous activities before he also abused them. He regularly slipped into the girls' shared bedroom and climbed into one or the other bed for sexual activities, without awakening the sleeping sister. Like many pedophiles, he defended his contemptible sexual abuse by advising the girls that he was preparing them for marriage.

Despite Celeste and Anne's compliance with Carlos' abusive demands, they were not spared other beatings or verbal humiliations from him. It was after many years of continual abuse before either sister realized that they had both been his sexual targets and even then the end of this abuse was nowhere in sight. While the Teitelbaum children were trying to cope with these terrors, mobster activities remained relentless.

Murder in the First Degree

Benjamin Siegel spent about four or five days at the ranch in 1947. He took over the secure bedroom next to the big garage and spent much of his time at the pool house. He and a woman friend had a private dinner every night without our family members bothering them. Even though the children were instructed not to disturb visitors like Ben, we sometimes connected at least briefly. They left after about one week.

Not long afterward, Pop returned to Florida to address legal matters related to Al Capone's death. My father led the press to believe that Capone died penniless. The only truth in that was there was no money in Capone's pants pockets at the moment of death. A powerful man, Capone left a legacy that outnumbered any monetary inheritance, and I was born in his shadow.

More bad news arrived shortly thereafter. On June 20, 1947, Pop received a phone call from Allen Smiley that Benjamin Siegel had been murdered. Smiley had been sitting near Siegel in Virginia Hill's house when the murder occurred, while Virginia was upstairs, out of harm's way.

Benjamin Siegel was buried at the Hollywood Cemetery next to Paramount Studios. His gravesite is marked with his name, birth and death dates, and the inscription, "From the Family". The inscription is a gruesome reminder about the deadly gifts anyone can expect from the mob, also known in Chicago as 'the outfit'. Benjamin's so-called friends disposed of him and left an undying reminder of their esteem for him on his gravesite.

Our family was intertwined with Capone and Siegel from my father's early years. Back at the Loveless Ranch, the Teitelbaum children tried to find comfort and safety wherever we could, not really knowing what we sought or how to find it. However, there were a few bright spots in this dark landscape.

Auntie Mom

Aunt Hannah was a very special person in my life. I was only two years old when Hannah began teaching me to read, write, draw, sing, and dance. Her belief, like Mother's, was that a person could do anything if they really wanted to as long as it began with a good education.

Hannah offered her loving guidance to me every day as my sisters and brother went to school. We walked the gardens and she taught me about plants and colors. She schooled me in ABCs. Using pencils or crayons, she patiently made sure that I understood each letter and eventually each word that I wrote. We read together from a series of Golden Books. This was an exciting time of discovery for me, creating fast bonds with my aunt and the wonder of education.

Each day when my sisters and brother returned from school, I loved showing them what I learned. They encouraged me and shared a little about what they were learning, too. Even though I was envious of their experiences, to this day I believe they would have preferred to stay home with our Aunt Hannah and me. There was something special and endearing about the way she mothered me.

In a short time, by the age of three and a half, I was reading books out loud, and later telling anyone who would listen the whole story in my own words. Mom was pleased that I could read stories to her at night and often encouraged my education, although she was busy running the entire ranch, paying the bills, participating in PTA, and generally choreographing all of the ranch activities. I always believed that I was going to get a great education, and my mother and Aunt Hannah were certain that I would make a great lawyer. While I didn't realize back then exactly what a lawyer did, I learned quickly that legal work contained specific perils all its own.

Hiding in Plain Sight

More than once, Mom cautioned all of her children that they were not allowed to reveal the names of the Teitelbaum clients. According to her instructions, disobedience to this family rule might easily lead to the entire family's death. Mom's wisdom, in retrospect, was rather shallow and frankly, downright twisted. Now I understand that there was just cause for our silence in those days; their clients were not just 'nice guys who dressed snappy' but truly nasty, ruthless killers who would not hesitate to bring harm to our house for slights real or imagined. But, this is a new day and those clients are all but dead and gone while I'm still here to tell this story.

The Teitelbaum clients, also knows as 'friends', included but were not limited to: Ralph and Al Capone, Chicago; Gabriel and Theresa Capone; Moses Annenburg; Benjamin Siegel; Joseph Greenburg; Jack Dragna and sons; Louie Romano; Jimmy Fratiani; Al Smiley (my father's best friend); Mickey Cohen; the Fader brothers and 'Uncle' Tony Arcado. Clearly, the Teitelbaum clients, represented by this partial list, would fill any hall of fame for criminal enterprises in the United States. Pop always said that even the worst people in the world are entitled to the best representation that money can buy. Representation apparently involved more than legal support.

Pop and his friends frequently climbed into the limo and were chauffeured by Carlos into Palm Springs or Cathedral City. Local police and sheriff department officials, many of whom were Pop's friends, ran card game houses in Palm Springs as well as a whorehouse in Cathedral City. The partyers and their bodyguards returned to the ranch late at night, gathered around the enormous well-stocked bar in the living room, and continued partying until the sun came up. Carlos and the other bodyguards, however, stood guard just outside the doors of the compound, along with the pack of guard dogs roaming around the fortress-like cement walls.

Other times, Pop would be gone for a couple of days. It was "all business," as Pop told Mom. Mom did not really want to know the details and we all knew the kind of business he was in but just stayed very quiet about it, especially when Pop was around. Since we were given clear instructions to 'never talk about family business' upon threat of death, we heeded that advice most explicitly.

The Loveless Ranch was a perfect escape for our parents' clients from harsh eastern winters of Chicago and New York. The compound was an isolated paradise where visitors felt comfortable talking openly, knowing they would never be heard by unfriendly elements.

The Guest

From 1946 to 1953 it was our family custom to escape the heat of the Indio summer by moving to Beverly Hills. Two or three weeks after Anne's birthday party, we moved to a large bungalow at the Beverly Hills Hotel to ride out the hot summer months of July and August, as was our annual tradition. The searing Indio heat was easily forgotten in the cool, elegant surroundings, complete with swimming pools, 24-hour food service, a beautifully painted cabana, and limo services. It was easy to make friends with other kids and families. We met many movie stars who also enjoyed lounging poolside.

Life was good and there were no obvious pressures. All animosity between Mom and Pop seemed to completely dissolve during this time and our sister, Linda, was born 9 months after our first summer break. Linda's birth on April 29, 1947, made her the new center of attention. With light brown hair and dark eyes, Celeste, Anne, Albert, and I adored her. All of our family members and many of our friends flocked to the house from around the country to see and welcome Linda.

The harmony between Mom and Pop seemed to hold for now, which might have been due to the fact that Pop was having problems with Roxanne. There were many stories about her drunken rages, knife-wielding threats, and bizarre parenting behaviors. Pop's original family, his first family, was glad to share their love with him and we were sure that he was right where he belonged – at home with us.

Abe Bernstein was one of Mom's very, very close friends from Chicago. Soon after Linda's birth, he came to visit us at the ranch from Chicago, where he had deep connections with the mob. During his visit, Abe pulled Pop aside and told him to take care of his first family. It was, quite ironically, a lecture on morality and responsibility, a concept essentially foreign to both men. The word from Aunt Hannah was that Pop agreed in person, but evidently his fingers were crossed behind his back during the responsibility promise that Abe extracted from him. Deceit much more accurately reflected Pop's nature than fidelity.

Guns and Dogs

The Loveless Ranch was well protected by our five guard dogs. They randomly roamed within the eleven-foot high walls almost every night to dissuade uninvited guests. No intruders ever came all the way into the compound.

However, one evening Carlos sounded an alert that intruders were heard just outside of the big wall. He appeared to engage them in a gunfight and released all of the guard dogs from their kennel to give chase. Shots were fired but no interlopers were ever captured; not a drop of blood was found in spite of the number of shots fired and not one of the dogs appeared to have a bloody muzzle resulting from an attack on any intruder. The outcome of the event leads me, in retrospect, to wonder whether there were actually any trespassers at all, or whether Carlos staged the 'intrusion' with another plan in mind.

Immediately thereafter, Mom asked Carlos to move into the big ranch house so he could better protect all of us. Some would say she just let the dog in. Others would agree with me and say that he engineered the invitation by carefully staging an intrusion. Carlos shared a room with Albert for many years. Even after moving into a different bedroom, Carlos always kept some of his belongings in Albert's room. One of these belongings was a gun, which eventually became a deadly threat to Carlos and nearly cost my own freedom down the road.

Dangerous Liaison

In 1947 or maybe even earlier under the radar, Aunt Hannah entered a common law relationship with Carlos, who was 15 years her junior. She later called him her 'Charles Bronson.' In retrospect, however, I believe that their relationship represented his desire to enter our family in order to increase his status in the Coachella Valley. Given Carlos' background and violent tendencies, it is no surprise that Hannah and Carlos had an extremely volatile relationship. He kept knocking her down, literally, and she kept getting up.

I assumed Hannah and Carlos were married about this time and didn't understand anything about common law marriages. After moving in with her, Carlos removed his chauffer cap and refused to ever wear it again. Additionally, he insisted on being called 'Uncle' Carlos, something I never did. I always saw him only as the man who made my life particularly miserable as the years went on, nothing more than the foreman of the Loveless Ranch who could wield a bullwhip with the ease of a boxer's punch.

Although Hannah was caring and loving with my older siblings and me, I never saw Hannah and Carlos express any kind of affection toward each other. I relished her attention and could barely tolerate his presence. Instead of affection, their style of connection was commanding and explosive. When it was clear that they had become a couple, my jealousy and disgust were triggered every time I saw them together.

Polio

To lighten the load on Hannah, a new governess named Lizette was hired to care for me when I was 3 years old. She always dressed in a starched white uniform and a matching white jacket. Whenever she was outside in the sun, she also wore a straw hat decorated with a white bow. Her hair was chemically blonde, just like Aunt Hannah, she had pasty white skin, a straight nose, and a pointy chin. I even remember her smelling a little bit like Campbell's tomato soup.

She tired easily from chasing me around the compound so she resorted to putting me in a large, black, four-wheeled tram. I didn't mind being rolled around the ranch, over to the tennis courts, and then out to the rumpus room by the pool.

All I had to do was tell Lizette where I wanted to go and she rolled me to that location, as though she was my personal chauffeur. If I was hungry, she rolled me into the kitchen. If I was sleepy, she rolled me under a huge grapefruit tree where she fanned the flies away from me while I napped. Flies never landed on any of the Teitelbaum children when Lizette was around.

This went on for about two months until my mother intervened and asked why I was always in the tram. Lizette lied and told Mom that I had been complaining about my legs hurting whenever I walked, instead of telling the truth that I was extremely difficult to corral.

Mom immediately called Dr. Ralph Pauley, a general practitioner in Indio, so I was sent directly to the hospital where I was given a spinal tap. The medical staff explained that they were checking me for polio. The tests were negative, however, the spinal tap left a nasty red circle from the bottom of my spine up to the middle of my back. During my convalescence from the procedure, I climbed out of bed, up onto the dresser, and looked into a full-length mirror where I saw the extent of the bruising damage.

I was never returned to the tram and Lizette was let go. In her place, a younger and more energetic governess, also in a white suit, was hired. She was very capable of chasing after me and I certainly gave her a run for her money!

The tram was kept near my mother's room to be used for my infant sister, Linda. Whenever I saw the tram or whenever people threatened to put me into it again, I reacted by running away and hiding in order to avoid another traumatic spinal tap. It turned out that any confinement became associated with trauma for me. Meanwhile, my parents were on the verge of a big win that would send them traveling the entire country.

The Big Win

In December of 1947 Pop received a phone call from Allen Smiley, who told Pop about a horse from upstate New York that was a long shot. He guaranteed that it would win but wanted to keep secret the fact that it was a fixed race. When Al asked Pop to act as a surrogate and place a $1,000 bet to win through a bookie on his behalf, Pop asked if he might also lay a bet, and Smiley laughed out loud saying, "Do what you want!" Pop called his bookie in Chicago, who said it would take awhile to see if the bets could be placed. My father was never one to wait, so he called the next bookie, and the next, and the same story was repeated for about three hours, involving no less than twenty different bookies.

Fifteen minutes before the race went off Pop's phone never stopped ringing. Each of the bookies confirmed Pop's $2,000 bet to win. My Pop was quite a gambler, placing an ultimate bet of forty thousand in two thousand dollar increments on that horse to win. Allen Smiley's contribution was a mere $1,000 of the entire bet.

Within minutes of the bookies confirming his bets, the buzz was out in Chicago that Pop was on to something big in that race, and one his clients immediately turned on the wire connected directly to Pop's office. The race was transmitted live, just in time for Pop to hear all of the details. The horse won, making Al Smiley a satisfied man with $8,750 in winnings and Pop was the happy recipient of approximately $340,000.

Gathering all of the winnings together would have been difficult or impossible from a distance, so Mom and Pop packed up for a collections trip, Mom with her hatbox for storing the money and a particular resolve to bring her own share of the money back home. They spent the next three months on a first class train with their bodyguard, Louie Romano, to convince all of the bookies to settle their debts without a challenge. They traveled from San Diego to Maine, Florida to Seattle, and sixteen stops in between.

When not between cities, they stayed in first class hotels or with friends. They collected earnings from all over the country. Every bookie was too afraid not to pay up on the debt, especially because 'Uncle' Louie was a very 'serious' man who did not play games. This was definitely a two-hatbox trip because $340,000.00 in cash takes up a large amount of space. The trip itself ended in a terrible tragedy for the entire Teitelbaum family, every one of whom was shaken to the core.

Chapter Five: 1948

Death of Innocence

In March 1948, while Mom and Pop were out collecting the last dregs of their $340,000 in gambling winnings, Aunt Hannah decided to visit her sister, Rose, in San Francisco. Perhaps she needed a break from Carlos, but who really knows? My Aunt Chane and Aunt Norma were asked to come to the ranch to help watch my siblings and me. Aunt Chane traveled by train with my cousin Roger from Chicago while Norma made the short drive from Los Angeles. In addition to watching over us, Aunt Chane, who was the older of the two sisters by a mere two years, was also asked to keep an eye on Carlos and the rest of the ranch staff including the cooks, maids, and ranch hands.

There was a powerful strain of influenza, related to bird flu, running through the Coachella Valley and the rest of the country in 1948. Albert, Celeste, and Anne, all in school at this time, were the first of the Teitelbaum children to catch this virus. The virus quickly spread to Linda and me, who shared a playpen together. While each of us was quite sick, Linda was the sickest of the five of us and continued to weaken, eventually developing pneumonia.

When Albert, Celeste and Anne got sick, Aunt Chane called Aunt Hannah in San Francisco. Hannah said she would return immediately but post-war transportation being what it was, the trip would take two full days. Immediately after Dr. Pauley determined that Linda developed pneumonia, telegrams were sent to Mom and Pop who were also determined to rush back home as fast as possible, a trip that would take two to three days.

I remember Aunt Chane as a strong, no-frills, take-charge woman who, alongside her younger sister, Norma, was placed in a nearly impossible situation. Dr. Pauley was called to the house during times when doctors made house calls, to examine the five Teitelbaum children along with Roger and many of the adults at the ranch. He prescribed treatments for each of us. He determined that Linda was the most vulnerable because of her age and her deteriorating condition.

The next day, Dr. Pauley returned to the house and insisted that Linda should be taken to the hospital because of her severe respiratory symptoms. Aunt Chane, who was the sister in charge, believed that a steam tent along with 24 hour nursing care at home would be as effective as hospital treatment. The steam tent was a typical Melnick family cure, learned from Grandma Tillie. Apparently, Dr. Pauley reluctantly acquiesced to Chane's plan so long as there was nursing care present at all times. Aunt Chane and Aunt Norma also took turns watching over Linda and the other children.

Nurses cycled pots of boiling water underneath the make shift tent constructed of bed sheets to maintain sufficient steam in order to ease Linda's breathing. During the first night shift, a second nurse took over and eventually fell asleep on duty. Both of my aunts were exhausted from caring for so many sick children all day long and were likely developing signs of the flu themselves as well. Late that night, Aunt Chane came to Linda's room and found the nurse sleeping in a chair. Linda lay lifeless under a sheeted tent. She died sometime on Friday night, March 19, 1948.

A huge commotion erupted among all of the adults in the house at the time. Storming into my room and shaking me, Aunt Chane began screaming hysterically, "Not my little girl!" She continued shaking me while yelling in my face, "It should have been you!" At not quite four years old, I could not clearly comprehend the problem; though I knew something terrible had happened. While still suffering from the flu, I was thrust into fear and confusion. Nothing made any sense at all. The only thing coming through that night was that somehow Linda was gone. I have come to believe that Aunt Chane was shattered, she was devastated, and took it out on me.

Blame for Linda's death was kicked around from person to person; there was enough blame to go around. Aunt Chane blamed and subsequently fired the nurse. Aunt Hannah later told us that the steam tent was still working and there was nothing in the house that could have helped Linda. Hannah argued that Dr. Pauley's instruction to send Linda to the hospital was correct. What is clear, however, is that Aunt Hannah wasn't back at the ranch to engage in the conversation between Aunt Chane and Dr. Pauley, as she was still traveling back to the ranch when Linda died. Aunt Norma, as usual, remained neutral on the entire tragedy with the exception that she consistently questioned the wisdom of her sister, Esther, who was conspicuously absent from her children.

It is thought that Aunt Chane originally learned the steam-tent remedy from Grandma Tillie. The family story goes something like this. When Uncle Alvin, Tillie's sixth child, appeared to be still-born in 1911, the doctor said there was nothing that could be done to save him. Instead of letting the baby go, Tillie said she knew better. To save her son, she immediately massaged Alvin's chest until he was revived and then kept him under a steam tent. Alvin survived and lived a long life. Other family stories attribute the method to Grandma Tillie's home remedy for colds and flu.

In the final analysis, there was plenty of blame to go around. It seems that Mom's sisters all tended to point the finger at Chane with the exception of Norma who decided that neutrality was what was needed in order to keep the peace. Chane evidently internalized that criticism, never mentioning the matter again. In fact, that silence extended to Chane's children, who only learned of Linda's existence and death when they became young adults.

Mom and Pop returned home from Florida on Saturday after receiving first a desperate telegram and then a confirming phone call. When Linda died they were still on the train. None of the children, who were still suffering themselves from the flu, were allowed to attend Linda's funeral. Even though I was three and one-half years old when that tragedy occurred, I still to this day think Linda is around. Our innocent sister, Linda, was buried only fifty feet away from Pop's friend, the notorious Benjamin Siegel, in the old mausoleum of the Hollywood Cemetery.

At least once every month during all the time we remained at the ranch, I went into Linda's bedroom, sat on the spot where she died, and spent a little time there. I talked out loud to her and always hoped to hear a reassuring response. Try as hard as I could over the years to communicate with Linda and hear her sweet voice in return, she never once reassured nor comforted me.

I still visit the old Hollywood Mausoleum and place flowers there for Linda. Her death and Aunt Chane's words, "It should have been you", continue to haunt me; what I have come to realize is that those words, which I took personally, were the cries of a hysterical woman in the moment of terrible despair. That being said, what I know now is different than my emotional response to this complex heartbreak. My consolation is the lasting knowledge that Linda did not have to suffer through the next 11 years of terror, including vicious attacks on innocent bodies and tender souls. In my heart I know with certainty that Linda would have been next in line for the same attacks and humiliation that the rest of us suffered. Those horrors still affect each one of us to this day.

Dissolving the Deal

Mom and Pop's relationship became more difficult and even alienated after Linda's death. Pop already had two children with his new family. Mom retreated into her well-appointed bedroom and stayed there almost exclusively. Mom could not stop grieving for her daughter, Linda, and for the love of her life, Pop. We still saw my Pop at least once a year after that, usually around a holiday. He was scheduled to spend a week with us each year, but always left within three or four days instead. Other times he showed up for unannounced visits, which completely delighted all of us. It didn't seem fair that Pop was around for so much more of my brother Albert's life than for my own, especially because I loved him so much.

We knew something was seriously wrong with our mother. My brother and sisters continued to go to school rather independently and I studied with Aunt Hannah who had become the resident mother figure. We continued calling her "Auntie Mom." Since I spent most of the day at home, I bonded with Aunt Hannah more than the other children did. She and I were inseparable and our love ran deep.

My Safety Net

Over the years Aunt Hannah saved some of my childhood innocence from the harshness of reality. She cared expertly and lovingly for me in many ways during this period. Aunt Hannah taught me about different types of roses and rocks. She also taught me how to grow plants and wisely warned me not to eat all the big, fat, ripe blackberries growing up a 40 foot wall between the great white wall and the five room house until after everybody else had some. Mom was at home physically, but she was unable to protect herself or her children, let alone communicate regularly with us. She lost all interest in the world.

During the times when Mom was essentially isolated, Aunt Hannah took the place of Mom in our lives for all practical purposes. She provided a safety net for my siblings and me even though there was a significant unspoken conflict because of her relationship with Carlos. Resolving their relationship was something like being caught in an emotional trap without any clear path out. However, I was and remain grateful for the care and love provided by Aunt Hannah during those unbelievably difficult times. My relationship with her and the good times shared with other family members were the breath of life for me.

Family Convergence

During the summer of 1948, following Linda's springtime death, we started a tradition that lasted about six years. Most of our extended family members converged on the ranch and stayed anywhere from two to three weeks. It was crowded during those gatherings, with various combinations of visitors from my extended family, including four grandparents, ten aunts, eight uncles, and twenty-three cousins. When everyone was in the swimming pool, it exploded with water fights, near drowning, cannonballing, and other foolish actions. Children and adults alike showed off in diving expositions, with sun so hot that it could bring on a sunburn within fifteen minutes. White vinegar and baking soda were mixed into a paste and used as the universal cooling remedy for sunburns. On certain days the entire clan smelled seriously like an Italian salad, minus the basil.

Every bedroom was full to overflowing with relatives each summer. The kitchen was busy around the clock, regardless of the hour, and the maids were running after everyone trying to keep the house clean. Our ranch hands kept the grapefruit orchard and date groves freshly disked, turning the hard, sandy soil over so that it was soft and well tended for children to run and play.

Several drivers, including Carlos, took tandem car trips into town for ranch guests who wanted to shop or watch a movie at the Aladdin Theater. Townspeople were always pleased with the patronage they received from my relatives during those outings.

On our birthdays, entire school classes with their parents and other family members came over to our house for pool parties. We served a wide variety of elegant hors d'oeuvres, barbeque items, and pastries. Even PTA parties were held at night with the compound all lit up and dazzling. City Councilmen and Mayors from around the Coachella Valley asked to throw events at the ranch. Governor Knight showed up for some of the festivities. The Loveless Ranch was the showcase of our valley, at least during these years, and at least from the outside. Unfortunately, all that sparkles is not golden.

Within the first year after Linda's death, Mom was pregnant again. At age 45, she carried the baby boy full term, but he was reportedly stillborn. The situation was just considered to be matter of fact. There was no expression of sorrow or loss. Instead, life went on as usual. Mom remained in silent isolation in her bedroom. In the Teitelbaum family, it now seemed like children's lives held no value and received no compassion. We went through the motions of family life and there were moments of playful levity, but a solid foundation of love and respect was wanting.

The Hamster Invasion

When I was almost four years old, we left the Beverly Hills Hotel in a brand new 1949 black Cadillac limousine to return home following a summer reprieve from Indio's scorching heat. Each one of us had a new pet hamster to bring home with us. The house had been prepared for our arrival by a team of maids and cleaning crews. Our ranch hands built a huge wooden maze for the four pets. The maze was even bigger than the train set in my room, which had been mounted on plywood and measured approximately 4 feet by 8 feet.

Within six months the hamster population had increased from four to sixteen. By the next year they had increased to a dangerously high census, around forty or fifty hamsters. That was when the great hamster escape occurred.

The industrious little creatures first chewed and then burrowed through the wooden maze, wandering freely throughout the ranch house. Somehow they found their way to create nests in the walls, which gave people the shivers just to hear them scratching about. On the bright side, the hamster invasion caused all of the rats to move away from the house and back out into the date groves.

Years later, while watching television late at night in the den with the television screen light bouncing off the green linoleum floor, the silhouette of an entire hamster herd would be illuminated, scampering across the floor, and disappearing into another wall. We delighted in jumping up, pouncing on their fat scurrying bodies, and collecting the slow, tardy, and stray among them. Although we corralled the prisoners in a metal cage to prevent further escapes, we never succeeded in capturing all of the renegades, nor could the feral cats.

Most of the hamsters remained more effective in their stealth avoidance and evasion techniques than any of the Teitelbaum children. There were no walls, no cracks, and no escape routes for us. We had no place to hide.

Wild Cats

Somewhere between fifty to one hundred wild cats and kittens occupied the ranch land. There were always baby kittens somewhere on the compound. Sometimes our guard dogs killed those feral cats, but most of the felines were generally able to care for themselves. Also, they helped control the groves' resident rodents. Any time rodents found their way into the house, we quickly cleaned and befriended a few cats, who returned the favor and paid their respects by patrolling, chasing, catching, and eliminating mice indoors. The gangster parallels are not lost on me. It's all about survival of the fittest, paying respects, and doing favors for each other.

Love Leaves Town

One day just before my fourth birthday, Aunt Hannah called the children together and told us she had to leave for a while. What's more, she said that she was leaving that very day. All of us were very confused and desperately sad; nobody was more upset than I was. There was no explanation whatsoever about her sudden departure. Even at my young age, I already knew that it was not safe to ask questions, so along with my siblings I remained quiet in the face of this enormous loss.

Aunt Hannah wore a blue skirt, a white blouse, a thin brown jacket, and a small brown hat on that sad day. She carried one old brown wicker suitcase. After she kissed and hugged us all, Hannah climbed resolutely into a car and drove away with Carlos. From my perspective she was not the same Aunt Hannah who taught me to read and write. She looked sad as she got into the car; tears welled up in the corners of her eyes. We were not to see her again for quite a few months.

When Hannah left the ranch, I grieved for her every day and felt a profound sense of loss. She had been my chief cheerleader and protector. Of course, I survived and even learned to stand up to my brother somewhat during Hannah's absence. He was still hitting both of my sisters and me on a regular basis. Every time he passed by, he punched us on the arm or slapped us on the back. It wasn't a friendly kind of greeting at all. Celeste also hit Anne and Anne hit me. I was the end target, the bottom of the pecking line, for everyone!

Christmas - Who Would Know?

Aunt Hannah's absence from the ranch made things seem upside-down. Birthdays and other celebrations were far less exciting. Without her smile to uplift our spirits, everything seemed far less interesting. This was especially true as the winter holidays approached.

Our family always indulged in purchasing huge Christmas trees in spite of the fact that we were Jewish. There was never a question about the conflict in our religious heritage created by the presence of a Christmas tree. At the Loveless Ranch, twenty-five foot tall trees were placed in the living room, reaching all of the way up to the cathedral ceiling. They were cut especially for us up past Hwy 74 in Idyllwild.

Every year the decorated Christmas tree, all lit up, was stunning. Presents were stacked high enough to completely obscure the fireplace behind the tree. We invited friends to join our family in the holiday festivities. Carlos' brothers and sisters who lived and worked at the ranch also participated. Christmas dinner was followed by gifts for all. Those were happy times.

Mother once received a Christmas card and after reading it she asked, "Who is this Felix Navadad? Does he work for us?" She was completely naive about the joke she just made. By now even I knew how to say Merry Christmas in Spanish. My mother, however, never bothered to learn Spanish despite the large number of Spanish speaking help on the ranch and the resident population of Indio. By contrast, my father was literate with Greek, Portuguese, Italian, French, Spanish, German, Yiddish, and English.

The Year to Forget

The year 1948 was filled with traumatic experiences for me. The death of my sister Linda in March, Mom hiding out in her room, and Aunt Hannah abandoning us in September; the collective experiences were difficult for the entire family and me. Carlos, without the Aunt Hannah's positive influence, became even more violent and abusive as we entered the New Year. Despite small islands of happiness when I was free from trauma, 1948 was a year I would forget if I only could.

Chapter Six: 1949

Food Wars

Over the course of my mother's many physical and emotional absences, Aunt Hannah had always there for me, to act as mother when Mom was nowhere to be found. She read with me every day, and always managed to bring a bit of light to even the darkest times. As an adult reflecting upon my own childhood, I believe she took that gift of maternal surrogacy too far under the circumstances. I developed a false sense of security in our relationship and was devastated by her tendency to excuse the abuse that was routinely leveled at her and at others whom she loved. I was also devastated by her absence.

Hannah had always been the first one to hug me and to make sure that I was served enough food at dinner. She intervened when my older brother and sisters tried stealing food off my plate. Since Aunt Hannah was no longer at the table, I picked up food with my hands and used my fork to fend off food thieves. With ten people eating together, I learned early on to use my fork as a defensive weapon. Others liked to help themselves from my plate if I did not eat fast enough. Even dinnertime at the Teitelbaum house was an aggressive, invasive, boundary battle. I still eat fast today, as though a 'fast' eating switch froze completely in the 'on' position during those difficult days.

Who is In and Who is Out?

Before I was in kindergarten, I knew that my Pop was an important man, almost larger than life, and that he was a lawyer representing 'family friends.' The fact is I had no real understanding about what it meant to be a lawyer or what kind of people Pop represented. My brother and sisters frequently said that Pop and Mom were Al Capone's attorneys and that they defended gangsters in Chicago and around the country. My siblings also seemed to get lots of attention by telling their classmates stories about Pop and Mom. After all, how many kids could say their parents were mob lawyers?

Even though I did not know exactly who Al Capone was, I treasured the golden gift that he sent on the occasion of my birth. It remained in its original blue felt box over the years. There was a special place for it in my dresser, covered by a hollow bottomed music box that I painted yellow with Aunt Hannah's help. My initials, RT, were painted in black over the yellow base coat.

I learned what it meant that my Pop was a lawyer for gangsters by watching movies like "White Heat" with James Cagney, and realized that the "friends" he represented had no respect for human life or the law. As young as I was, I began to understand that my Pop used his skills to manipulate the law to conform to the interest of his clients, not something to be proud of for sure. All I could do to cope with that information was to make up silly, irreverent, and inappropriate songs about gangsters, Chicago, and murder. Those songs got me in a little trouble now and then but they helped me tolerate the frightening reality I was slowly beginning to understand.

Unless extended family members were present, Mom and Pop were fighting all the time, mostly about the company that Pop kept, but not always; sometimes the fights were about money. Pop often scheduled two-week stays at the ranch, but when the arguments started Pop climbed into the limo and headed out to Vegas to visit Al Smiley and Benjamin Segal. Because Pop fancied Beverly Hills, our family spent a couple of months every summer at the Beverly Hills Hotel during the years 1946 to 1951. Later, we rented a house at 711 Beverly Drive when it was too hot to stay at the Indio ranch. Pop loved spending time with rich people in Beverly Hills.

Family tended to flock to the Beverly Hills house because we were close to Uncle Bernie's Toy Store and we could easily walk to see one of Pop's friends, Jimmy Durante, at his home just a few blocks down from our house. Pop also had friends at MGM and Fox Studios who took us to see movies and cartoons before they were released. The Beverly Hills summer respite lasted for a few years until our financial well ran dry. After that we just weathered the hot summers in the cool air-conditioned Indio ranch house. Like my father, I much preferred Beverly Hills.

Later on Pop bought a Beverly Hills home to share with his second family, located directly next to another Al Teitelbaum, who was a famous furrier. His furs were featured on many television shows and movies, along with credits noting, "Furs by Teitelbaum". One of the times when the FBI obtained a warrant to tap Pop's phone, they mistakenly tapped the wrong Teitelbaum. In so doing, they found out that the other Teitelbaum was also up to no good. He was imprisoned for insurance fraud and later released when his debt was paid off. It was almost a consolation prize for the bumbling federal officers.

Flaws in the Ruby

Despite or maybe because of all the home-life transitions and trauma, Celeste was smart enough in school to usually earn "A plus" on every assignment. When the occasional 'B' grade showed up on an assignment, she put her nose back into the books and reclaimed her rightful 'A.' She was very strong in body but was often upset about what seemed like imagined wrongs, and was commonly known as a tattletale. Celeste was always grumpy and mean; the reason behind her anger was beyond me. However, at least two others in the house knew very well and were shamefully responsible for the injustice that provoked her anger.

Even so, Celeste had a good sense of humor and continued to collect chewed bubble gum in a giant ball, which grew over the years to about the size of a grapefruit. The maids would not go anywhere near that giant gumball to clean off the shelf where it rested; it simply stank to high heaven. Celeste's gumball, putrid as it was, represented the many layers of protection that she needed between herself and the toxic environment in which she lived; unlike Celeste, the gumball represented something untouchable, silently collecting the sins of constant abuse.

Celeste loved toys and porcelain dolls from around the world, which she and Anne received from our father and other family members. Anne and Celeste treated those dolls with respect, as the mobsters would say. After playtime, each doll was returned to its metal stand, and closely inspected to make sure the eyes could open and close on each small painted face. The girls' room was never a mess. In contrast to their damaged inner worlds, Celeste and Anne's dolls were pristine, well supported, and protected in an orderly environment.

My Corner of the World

In comparison to Celeste and Anne's well-appointed room, my room was always disorderly. Toys were everywhere. I had a huge chest of drawers with a mirror that went all of the way up to the cathedral ceiling. I slept in a king size bed next to a large window, which opened into the back yard and onto the tennis garden.

The back yard window was next to a large walk-in closet filled with toys, clothes, and those treasured green bookshelves with all my favorite Golden books. The bathroom had a shower, large bathtub, a tall toilet, and a sink with a big mirror. There were two steps in front of the sink so that I could climb up and see myself when I brushed my teeth. The wall on the other side of the room was covered with beautiful dark stained wood.

I had electric trains attached to plywood covering the room's green carpet. The twenty by twenty foot bedroom with cathedral ceilings was all mine. Friends came over to play with elaborate toys that were from Uncle Bernie's Toy Store, commonly accepted as the fanciest toy store in Beverly Hills. To outside eyes, my bedroom reflected an idyllic childhood environment.

I also loved each of the dogs that shared the ranch with us. There was Nicky the Doberman, Boy the Boxer, Scotty the Terrier, Copy the Shepard, and Rufus the half-coyote. There was Sandy, Floppy, Mazel the Cocker Spaniel, Pee-Wee, and Chico, a Chihuahua that my sister Celeste received for her birthday.

Ahead of My Time

Mom decided that I should start Kindergarten just before my fifth birthday. Hannah's tutoring had prepared me well, but we needed district approval for an age minimum exception. When the school district would not agree, Mom became unusually animated; she climbed out of bed and took me to school where she asked the board to interview me. The situation must have struck some chord in her 'helping the downtrodden' mission. Their questions were about basic reading and writing skills, so to their amazement, I walked over to a desk occupied by a Board Member, picked up a second grade reader and read it to them. Then I picked up a pencil and paper from the same desk and wrote out a story about how much I wanted to go to school so I could learn, grow up, and be anything I wanted to be. Finally, they agreed with Mom and I joined a kindergarten class at 4 years old, about one month shy of being 5.

The district representatives, however, advised Mom that I should be in a private school. We lived in Indio and the only private school option was in Los Angeles, which meant I would have to live with my Grandparents. Mother could not stand breaking up what was left of our Chicago-exiled family, so I began public school in Indio instead. Little did she know or seem to care about the dangerous fractures, which were already ripping our family apart from the inside out. If only Mom had agreed to let me live in Los Angeles, so many years of personal horror might have been escaped.

Friend and Foe

Since I had already learned to read and write, the kindergarten curriculum was boring, which caused my creative spirit to stray. I turned my attention toward making friends. It was easier said than done in my case. My older brother and sisters' presence already generated a wave of concern among the community because of wide spread knowledge about our parents' affiliation with Al Capone. Being driven to school in a big, black, 1949 Cadillac limousine did not help dissuade any parent's concerns.

My first experience with anti-Semitism occurred in school. Labels like Jew, bastard, and kike offended me to the core, so I countered them by learning to fight during my first month at school. I tutored myself in the fine art of self-defense by watching boxing and wrestling on television. In an effort to protect me, or perhaps to return herself to a more powerful and authoritative life, Mom became head of the PTA, which caused all of the parents to instruct their children in the fine art of walking lightly around each of the Teitelbaum children in order to avoid 'problems'. Some of the children simply turned their backs on me, as though I was not even present. It was a harsh reality for me to experience at such a tender age.

Heads Up!

During my kindergarten year I learned how deliberately cruel my twelve-year-old brother, Albert, really was. Albert was using our front lawn as a driving range and we made eye contact as I approached him across that green expanse. There was nothing at all cautionary in his gaze. He recognized my presence and deliberately asserted his power over me. When I leaned down to pick up a golf ball near Albert, he swung his six-iron and cracked my head open.

How could he have done such a horrible thing to me? As the family prince, everyone was expected to stay out of his way. He had been taught to feel a sense of entitlement about time, place, and person. The collision between his club and my head meant another emergency trip to Dr. Pauley's for seven stitches above my left eye. It still strikes me as peculiar that Albert never apologized and was never punished; it is one of the many events that make me wonder, to this day, about his ability to feel any empathy for others.

Much like Carlos, Albert never was called to account for his abusive actions. Also like Carlos, he had the freedom to walk away from any and all responsibility for his actions. Mostly he was not asked to explain himself and when he was confronted he always conveniently blamed his abuse on his victim. In the case of the golf club bashing in my head, he lied by saying that he never saw me. Even though I know otherwise, his lie was accepted as the truth of the matter.

Prodigal Aunt

As quickly as Aunt Hannah left, she returned within a year and seemed very happy to be back at home on the ranch with us; we were overjoyed that she returned to the family who loved her. However, she appeared to be somehow transformed in ways that were impossible for children to understand. Several years passed before the extent of that change was finally revealed. That being said, it was obvious to everyone that something between Hannah and Carlos had also been irrevocably altered. What had previously appeared to be subtle affection now became relentless and sometimes violent bickering. Aunt Hannah was overtly angry and the cause was as yet unknown to us.

The Teitelbaum clan seemed to engage in a repetitive dance no matter what the circumstances, which included two alternating steps: one step was either joyful or loyal and the second step was dangerous. Somehow we engaged whole-heartedly in joy and loyalty with abandon, regardless of the inevitable aftermath.

Take Your Vitamins

Right from the start in the Coachella Valley, Mom insisted that our Vitamin D should come from the sun. Her guidance was a shining example of maternal error. We are seafaring Ashkenazi Jews who came from Eastern Europe and are already olive skinned, but every Saturday Mom made us lie outside by the pool from 12 noon to 2 p.m., which turned our skin even darker. It was fortunate that none of us developed skin cancer, especially because Indio's temperatures can sometimes reach 120 degrees. Of course, while many people like to say "but it's a dry heat," you can take my word for it, to borrow a line from Robert Earl Keen, "It's hotter than a furnace fan."

On his first trip to the ranch in the summer of 1950, Uncle Harry was told by his wife, Aunt Florence, to cover up when he was outside so that he didn't get sunburned. He bragged, "Florence, I was in the tropics in the Army." His bravado was short-lived in the blistering heat; he turned as red as an apple. After being doused with the family's white vinegar and baking soda potion, Uncle Harry stayed inside the big house's refrigerated air conditioning for two weeks to recover from severe sunburn.

Safety in Numbers

One Thursday afternoon, all family members in residence piled into the limo with Carlos at the wheel and headed off to the Fairfax district, West Los Angeles, for the gathering of our tribe. We were celebrating Grandma and Grandpa's 50th wedding anniversary and everybody was there, even Uncle Ben, who emerged from his apparently forced isolation for this special occasion. Conspicuously missing, Uncle Felix stayed home in New York, running the Motion Picture Projectionist Union. Mom and Pop were fighting, as usual, so even though he showed up for the family photos, Pop exited immediately thereafter. Their current fight was about the money they had invested in my grandmother's house. Pop wanted the money back so he could have more cash in his pocket. Mom said no, it was a gift, so Pop answered by leaving the anniversary party.

We indulged in 3 days of endless celebrations with Grandma and Grandpa. All of our aunts and uncles were present and the dinners were filled with laughter; we ate large, played hard, and told family stories until the wee hours of the night. Children could be found sleeping in every nook and cranny of the house.

During the day, we took a couple of trips to the Farmers Market. On one such trip, cousin Roger, Albert, and I bought slingshots and each of us was having a great time shooting up cans, stop signs, streetlights, and such. Carlos caught us and told Roger he was going to get a beating.

Aunt Florence heard Carlos' threat, stepped in front of Roger and said loudly, "You will not lay a hand on these boys! Get away from them!" Carlos cringed and, like most cowards, backed away, but only after giving Albert a slap to his head. The rest of the weekend went smoothly at Third and Fairfax, including a trip to the movies on Saturday. Aunt Florence was the first and only person I ever saw back Carlos up without being knocked down to the ground. Her sainthood was confirmed for me on that most glorious day.

On Saturday night, approximately forty family members were seated indoors at a series of dinner tables, everyone honoring our grandparents with toasts. Stories were flying around the room about the old country, Chicago days, our parents, our earlier years, and our births. It was a treasure of family stories, lovingly repeated for the children to pass down to their own children. A photo was taken of everyone together, memorializing that blessed occasion.

Sunday was the cousins' special performance day. In the cleared out garage we put up curtains and held plays for our grandma and grandpa, aunts and uncles, and anybody else in the general vicinity. The performances lasted at least four hours. Some of the plays were great and some were not so great, unless you loved the performers. I did a hand farting performance, which I learned from the Sid Cesar Show, to the tune of "O Give me a Home where the Buffalo Roam." My rendition was met with some applause and also with many raised eyebrows. When the party ended, we sadly said our good-byes and prepared for a return to the reality of an abusive darkness. Good times were hard to find at the Loveless Ranch in Indio unless our relatives were in residence, mediating Carlos' reign of terror.

By the following Sunday night, fortunately, a legion of family members decided to return with us back to the ranch. Among the five or six family groups, I was closest to Aunt Florence's boys. We launched overstuffed lounge chair pads into the pool and had a great time floating on top of them until they became water logged and sank to the bottom of the deep end. It became necessary at that point to completely drain the pool and pull those soggy lounge pads out, since their water logged weight reached up to 100 pounds each.

During this visit my cousins and I found used cigarettes in Aunt Hannah's car and tried our hardest to light them. They were so old and stale, they simply fell apart, but the treasure hunt was very satisfying, indeed. Each summer for about four-years, Aunt Florence's family stayed with us for about three weeks at a time. Our antics somehow glued our relationships and we continue to delight in each other even decades later.

Date Night

There was not much light pollution in those days, so the stars and moon were bright, up close, and personal in the cool of the evening. Coyotes howled in the distance and just before sunset we sometimes tossed Medjool dates high up into the air to watch the tree bats dive, catch the dates, and then let them drop. The bats were tricked into thinking that the dates were enormous live insects. Sometimes they competed with each other to catch the flying prize.

Hundreds of bats swarmed the area each evening and helped reduce the local insect populations. Their reactions to our trick fascinated me and I loved playing this game of catch and release whenever I could. Even my dog, Rufus, joined in the fun on these warm evenings by howling back to the coyotes, who were actually his own distant cousins.

Festival of Dates

Between Lincoln's birthday and George Washington's birthday every year, Indio celebrated the Coachella Valley Date Festival for ten fun-filled days. The celebration included a carnival with a freak show, traditional carnival rides, and a wide variety of exhibit halls especially highlighting local produce, including dates and citrus fruit. There was a large stage for the traditional Scheherazade play and a queen was chosen to reign over the festival. Tens of thousands of people from all over the country, including local dignitaries, politicians, and Hollywood stars all converged to enjoy the event. In addition to fifty-cent kissing booths, camel races, and jockeys who directed ostriches with brooms, the festival boasted the best food on the planet; lemonade stands, colorful snow cones, cotton candy, fresh Mexican tamales, and hot peanuts.

I met both Bob Hope and Bing Crosby at the festival in 1951, when I was only six years old. Even at that age, I had already seen some of their movies. Bob Hope's unusual looks, generous spirit, and playful style all appealed to me. I fancied myself as his student, loved his adventures, and often fantasized about joining his travels.

A desert theme influenced the whole town, and most of the local citizens dressed up as Arabs for the festival. The Teitelbaum kids were no exception. Aunt Hannah and Mom got out the Singer one-stitch sewing machine and hired a seamstress to fit each of us from head to foot with exotic, authentic, Arabian garb. The costumes were beautiful and colorful, earning us a place on the festival parade floats with the Mayor and other dignitaries.

My brother and I volunteered to patrol atop the festival entrance, constructed to look like castle walls, in our Arabian uniforms with wooden swords. Our shift ended after two hours. After Albert left, I joined my friends for a few more hours of merry-making. My sisters volunteered at the date and citrus judging events, handing out blue ribbons before they took a turn at wandering around the event grounds. All locals in costume enjoyed discounted entrance fees and all of the food was very inexpensive. Two dollars could feed a child for an entire day with a little change left over. Why children would be left without adult supervision in a setting such as this is another discussion. Truthfully, the carnival was far safer than our own home.

We stopped going to the Date Festival in 1957. Even small amounts of money that might be spent at the fair became a burden on the family budget during some of the following years.

Halloween Prank and Sorrow

One October, Anne and Celeste were determined to dress me up for our local schools' Halloween contest, Ghosts and Goblins, in a costume fit to win the first prize. After an hour of failed attempts at creating just the right costume, Celeste and Anne took the 1890s clothing off of their life-sized doll. They dressed me in the doll's green satin formal gown with a gathered skirt, a bustle, and a matching bonnet. Anne found a dark brown curly wig, which they placed on my head. They made up my face as though I was from their doll collection and the transformation was dramatic.

At 5:00 PM, we climbed into the limo and headed to the Ghosts and Goblins competition, held at the Thomas Jefferson Junior High School. Not one soul, not even my friends recognized me under the curls, satin, and lace. I won the blue ribbon for second graders, dressed like an elegant lady from times gone by. Celeste and Anne, who did not win anything individually, were nonetheless very proud of their costuming and makeup artistry.

Following our return home, we went fully costumed into living room to say goodnight to Mom. When my mother saw me dressed up, she put her hands over her face in horror, dropped down into a chair, and could not stop crying. I imagine that my age and pretend gender must have reminded her of our lost sister, Linda. All three of us ran as straightaway into our rooms. Celeste and Anne stripped off my costume and redressed the doll as quickly as possible. We were all sick to our stomachs and confused; none of us had ever wanted to hurt our grieving mother. It's hard to say whether Mom was more traumatized by our actions than we were, because true to our family traditions, we never once spoke about the incident. However, Halloween completely lost its appeal to me as a result.

There were always community and family events to distract us from the traumas we experienced at home, we were masters at burying our feelings in a fast-paced environment and compelled to stay as busy as possible.

Party Lights

While Coke machines were installed around the front of the house, the coin functions were disabled so everyone could have as many free sodas as they wished. There were always a variety of carbonated choices, including Coke, Pepsi, Bubble Up, and Royal Crown (RC) Cola. The Ranch was all about partying.

During evening parties, my friends and I sometimes climbed the staircase to our sun deck, and then climbed over a barrier to crawl out onto the roof where we watched visitors mingling on the front lawn between the big house and the pool. We were mesmerized by the beautiful lights and by the visitors who danced between Mom and waiters bearing endless trays of food and drinks. Even though she was sequestered in her room during the day, Mom put on her best face and showed up for visitors during these events.

Sometimes we saw my brother and his friends running out of sight, or so they thought, into flower gardens behind the small green gate. From our vantage point on the roof, it was easy to see Albert, aged 15, and his friends join their girlfriends in the garden about 10 feet below us. Wide eyed, we watched everything and thought, "In seven more years, we will be hiding in the bushes, too!" The same scene was repeated over and over again. Under the big desert moon, away from the party lights, my brother and his friends were typical 1950s teenagers. I remember thinking about Abbott and Costello's skit: "Who is on first base?" Nobody slid into third base in these gardens, at least as witnessed by my friends and me from a most excellent vantage point.

Behind Mom's back, some of the party guests whispered about Mom and Pop's roles as Al Capone's attorneys. Mom was very aware of her reputation, so when Governor Knight asked one evening about who taught her to cook such great Italian food, without skipping a beat Mom said, "Al Capone's mother, Theresa". Mom was an expert at creating a perfect sand storm and she was pretty pleased with herself because of it. She loved telling this story over the years to anyone who would listen.

Fried Eggs

The Coachella Valley heat was scorching during the summer months, with normal temperatures ranging from 110 to 115 degrees. There were times when the temperature reached 120 followed by an episode of rain, which would hit the concrete in bursts of steam. The summer was so hot that we sometimes cracked eggs on the concrete to watch them cook. If we were distracted and looked away even for an instant, one of our dogs took only a split second to scarf down a tasty fried egg, as if we served as their personal short order cooks.

Since it was so hot, at least a foot of water evaporated daily from the pool, so I filled the cistern, opened the valves, and flooded the pool with fresh ice-cold water each day. We loved to cannonball into that refreshing swimming pool every chance we had.

During the other eight months at the ranch, temperatures were typically seventy to eighty-five degrees with cool mornings. At night the thermometers sometimes dropped so low that there was a thin layer of ice around the swimming pool.

Blood on the Floor

Playtime for the Teitelbaums usually involved swimming laps in the Olympic size pool. We practiced double flips, broke eardrums, and generally caused an abundance of water-based havoc.

When the pool was periodically drained and refilled, we perfected the fine art of diving into shallow water off the diving board. Sometimes there was no more than three to four feet of water in the deep end, even though the pool was 10 feet deep. Albert taught all of us how to dive headfirst into the water and then curve our bodies upward instead of smashing into the bottom. I scraped my chest and legs every now and again after misjudging the water's depth. This was such a frequent practice, it might be considered a mystery why no adult ever noticed or intervened, especially because of the extreme danger and the frequent superficial wounds. In context, however, there is no mystery at all.

Every one of the Teitelbaum children also loved fencing. With foil in hand and body armor in place, we dressed up and had a great time sparring with each other. We had all of the right equipment: pads, headgear, full white padded suits, foil tips, and judging cards. The four of us ran fearlessly at each other down canvas runways to strike. My mother once said somewhat proudly to the mayor of Palm Springs that the Teitelbaum kids were not playing "...if there was no blood on the floor." The boxer in her seemed delighted with this fierce competition.

Spontaneous Generation

It was also one hot afternoon in the summer of 1952 when Carlos and his sister, Maria, brought a sweet little girl who appeared to be about four years old into the ranch kitchen. Aunt Hannah, upon seeing the child, spontaneously screamed out loud in great surprise. We were all shocked at her outburst and didn't understand what was happening. The children were immediately ordered out of the house and into the date groves near the tennis courts, where we waited anxiously.

The child, Claudia, was later brought out to meet us in the groves. She did not speak any English at all, only Spanish. Completely overwhelmed and crying, Claudia was dressed beautifully, as if she was going to church, and Hannah was beaming with joy. Carlos and Hannah tried to introduce Claudia to me first, because I was the youngest. Amidst tears, Claudia continuously repeated only one Spanish word, 'vete', which means 'go'. Then Hannah picked her up and took her into the house.

It did not really matter to us that Claudia couldn't speak any English. We all helped her and soon she was bilingual. Sometimes it seemed like she would never stop talking. All of the children accepted her without reservation and she became just one of the tribe.

We later learned that Hannah recognized the little girl as her own daughter, given up at birth during Hannah's abrupt 1948 absence. Claudia joined our family shortly before the summer and within about one month she was in the middle of 50 relatives who came out for the summer holiday. Claudia was always with Aunt Hannah and we loved both of them dearly.

Another Fencing Accident

When I was almost seven years old and in the fourth grade, my brother, Albert, who was 13 years old, tried to abuse me. He took me into the bathroom and forced me to take off my clothes. Since I often ran around the house naked, I wasn't especially concerned at the time. Instead, I was pretty pleased that he was giving me some attention. He stripped down, too, and asked me if I knew what an erection was. I had never heard about an erection, so Albert showed me what he meant and then told me to bend over so he could show me what he could do with it. Just then Carlos broke the bathroom door off its hinges and proceeded to beat Albert into a pulp. Apparently Carlos thought Albert was stepping in on his territory.

As I was frantically putting my clothes back on, kneeling down and finishing up with tying my shoes, Carlos burst into the bathroom once more. This time he kicked me in my face, just above my right eye. Blood splattered across the walls and floor, so this time a trip to the doctor was unavoidable. Dr. Pauley took several stiches to close the gaping wound over my right eye. When the doctor asked how it happened, Carlos quickly replied, "It was just a fencing accident."

Over the years Dr. Pauley saw quite a few 'fencing accidents' in our family. So many accidents were left unreported that I often wondered how Dr. Pauley could overlook the appearance of physical abuse in our house. With a large number of adults who witnessed effects of rampant abuse at the Loveless Ranch, it is beyond me that not one of them ever had the courage to ask questions, let alone contact the authorities.

More Fireworks

On July 2, Carlos took me with him on a drive to Mexico for holiday supplies. I was surprised and very pleased that he would take me on a trip to buy firecrackers and even include a visit to his family. Before we went into his family's house, Carlos told me not to admire anything inside, as it would obligate his family members to give things to me, which he said was a Mestizo custom. I met many of his relatives, more brothers and sisters, and filled up on delicious tacos, chorizo, rice and beans, fresh tortillas, and loads of salad. Even better, I had a great time playing with the other children.

After the feast, we went into town and stopped at a store where Carlos was well known and obviously highly esteemed; they treated him like a king. He bought cherry bombs, M80s, and finger size firecrackers, all packaged together in a big brown paper bag. Carlos stuffed that bag with fireworks into the spare tire well, out of sight from border patrol authorities.

It was late afternoon when we were ready to come back across the border. The border guard asked if we had purchased anything. I looked at Carlos and said, "What about..." He stopped me with a nasty look and turned to the guard, saying, "Nothing, just visiting family." The guard waived us back into California for the long trip home.

I was tired and fell asleep in the front seat on the return drive. When I finally awoke, I was in the back seat; it was very dark outside and Carlos was driving. My clothes were off; I was completely naked. I felt confused and dazed like I had a heat headache, but I sat up and put on my underwear, pants, shoes, and socks. My shirt was torn at the armpit. I asked Carlos why my pants were off he replied gruffly, "Shut the fuck up!" and I did as he said. We returned to the Loveless Ranch and I went immediately off to bed. There was never another word spoken, never an explanation, and never an acknowledgement of any transgression.

Once again on Anne's Fourth of July birthday we celebrated with an abundance of fireworks. Albert and Carlos lit all of them. They covered lit cherry bombs with empty one-pound Maxwell house coffee cans. When the bombs exploded, the cans were blown up high into the air. There were so many different ways to set off explosives at the Loveless Ranch and it was strangely refreshing when the fireworks exploded in plain sight.

Chapter Eight: 1953

Give the Dog a Bone

One Saturday, Carlos decreed that everybody was grounded except for me. It wasn't clear what transgressions had occurred to cause the grounding, and we weren't ever allowed to question his authority anyway. He commanded and we complied. Period.

Since I was the only child not being punished, I was allowed to attend a movie alone for the first time. With popcorn and an orange soda, I sat in the lodges by myself at the Aladdin Theater in Indio. I watched a series of cartoons, the News of The Day, a Three Stooges short, and then "Twenty Thousand Leagues Under the Sea." This was a special day for me, and those movie tunes remain fondly in my musical repertoire.

After the movies were over, I called home and Carlos picked me up in the limo. As usual, I sat in the back seat. However, when I got home, I couldn't understand why none of my siblings would talk to me; it was as if I had done something wrong. During that afternoon while I enjoyed popcorn, orange soda, and the movies, Carlos sexually abused both of my sisters.

This was nothing new at the Loveless Ranch. None of us ever spoke the words of abuse out loud. Like many households where abuse was commonplace, we kept secrets even from ourselves. Silence, a form of anger turned inward, was a constant companion for each of the Teitelbaum kids.

Free Like Tarzan

It was about 4:00 p.m. that same day when Carlos told me to go out and play, as everybody was still grounded. I obeyed as always, feeling sad and alone but completely clueless about the circumstances or even about my feelings. I went into the garage and found a rope with one end tied to the rafters. I played Tarzan by tying the free end around my waist in a slipknot. Instead of swinging from branch to branch, I started swinging from a bench to a ladder and then to the station wagon.

Eventually, I missed the mark and was left hanging about three feet off the ground by a rope with a slipknot cinched tightly around my waist. It almost squeezed the life out of me! I was left hanging like that until dark when my sister, Anne, found me and cried out for help to cut me down. I was cut down by Aunt Hannah and taken to Dr. Pauley, who said I was hurt but not damaged.

The next day Carlos took me back to garage, cut a long piece of rope, and said, "So, you like to play with rope!" He grabbed my right hand, twisted my wrist, and pulled up to lift me off the ground, then started whipping me on my back and legs. Each time that thick rope hit my skin it felt like fifty angry bees stinging me. He must have hit me about twelve times before he was done, all the while holding me up, off the floor by my right wrist.

I tried to not yell out or cry but tears came anyway and eventually I also started screaming. All I could hear, though, was just the sound of that rope smacking me over and over again. Thick red welts rose up across my back and my legs and my wounded skin turned black and blue over the next couple of days. Of course, I was sure that it was my fault and I deserved the punishment. Like Anne and Celeste before me, I never spoke of the matter until now. I really wasn't trying to kill myself. I just wanted to be as free as Tarzan.

Target Practice

Carlos, Albert, and I sometimes dumped household trash together. We drove the tractor into our private date groves where ranch hands dug a disposal hole about eight feet deep and twenty-five feet long. After we emptied garbage into the hole and doused it with a gallon of gasoline, we set it on fire and stood by in case of any sparks ignited elsewhere. Water tanks were kept on the site in case of emergency.

There was a tree branch hanging down about twenty-five feet away, so Carlos and Albert started tossing big dirt clods at that target. I was left to watch the fire while they kept tossing and missing. They just could not hit the branch, so I put down the water tank and hose I had been holding and looked around.

Once I found just the right sized dirt clod with small rocks embedded into it, I used all of my strength and heaved that clod just as hard as I could. It lofted into an excellent ark and, to my amazement, hit the target square on. Albert and Carlos were not at all amused at the competition they just received from a little nine-year-old boy. They started hitting me instead of the branch with dirt clods, climbed onto the tractor, took off, and left me alone in the date groves. It was about a one-half mile walk back to the main house. Even though I very angry about having been abandoned, I still felt pretty proud of myself for hitting the branch.

Later that afternoon, Carlos took Albert and me to Foster Freeze in town for ice cream and root beer floats. It was Carlos' indecent practice to reward us after exercising his brutal control over any one of the Teitelbaum children. To us kids, things usually seemed a little better after that. It was, of course, only the surface that shined.

Canine Solace

During the most troubling times, after being punched, abused, kicked, and emotionally or spiritually drained, I often hid with the dogs in the dog pen outside the kitchen. They comforted me when nobody else could or would.

Most of the dogs stayed at the far side of the pen but there was large palm tree near the back of the house where I liked to sit in the sand, hidden from the rest of the world. Nicky lay down close to me, and Rufus sat behind me with his head on my shoulder. Nicky pushed in closer to me as if the two dogs were holding me, and then I cried. I sobbed with them holding me and me holding myself together while also leaning on them. I sobbed all the way down from the depths of my chest and could not seem to stop crying for the life of me. My tears were endless in that desert of a home, while Nicki and Rufus closed in more and more to protect me as best they could.

The dogs and I stayed together that way until my tears ran dry. Then I got up and played with all nine of the dogs at the same time. I loved to lie down on the sand and roll around with them, as though the weight of the world was not on my shoulders. From third grade to the end of seventh grade, the dog pen was the only safe place for me, sheltered among Rufus, Nicki, Boy, Sandy, Floppy, Mazel, Peewee, Blackie, and Chico.

Gallows Humor

To anyone looking in from the outside, the Loveless ranch was idyllic. Date groves surrounded the house. One could pick breakfast from the grapefruit trees most days, go for a swim in the pool in the morning, and go riding through the desert on the back of a beautiful horse named Nicky in the afternoon. Yes, the horse was also named Nicky, just like my dog.

The horse corral sat in the middle of the date grove, just far enough from the house to mask smells associated with the barn. Nicky came with the ranch as did the ranch hands who worked there. She was beautiful, standing six hands tall with a sleek brown coat and white markings on her feet and shoulders. I loved that horse so much; I visited her every single day.

If I wanted to go riding, I simply asked one of the ranch hands to saddle her up since I was too little to hoist the heavy saddle onto her back. But once on the horse there was no better rider; not either of my sisters or even my older brother could ride like I could. I was a natural and became known for my riding abilities.

Nicky was with us for five more years at the ranch. I fed her oats and pushed hay into her stall every day. On most days I brought her an apple or a few carrots as a special treat. On certain days I even brought her both. I never knew what treats my sisters or brother brought her but spoiling Nicky was never ever a concern.

There were times when Carlos hoisted Celeste, Anne, and me on Nicky's back and we all rode her together. There was even a time when Anne and my cousin Roger spread a picnic blanket underneath Nicky, in her shade, and had a little party lasting long enough for Carlos to discover these two six-year old kids under the horse. He disciplined the two of them right on the spot, and Roger couldn't sit down for a week from that whooping.

While I fed her and brought her treats, ranch hands who were all Carlos' brothers, did the real dirty work. They were responsible for mucking Nicky's stall, washing and grooming her, and seeing that she was well maintained. Because of their efforts, Nicky looked like a champion every single day.

On a particularly sultry summer afternoon, during one of those flash thunderstorms that are common on the Mohave Desert, a rather close bolt of lightning and a resounding clap of thunder spooked Nicky. She jumped out of her stall and then out of the corral, running wildly around the ranch. Her frightened whinnies could be heard from inside the house where we sought refuge from the storm, playing games and running around laughing and giggling as kids often do.

Carlos came into the room where my sisters and I were playing. "Don't you kids move," he ordered, "I've got some business I have to attend to outside." He left. We played. I don't know where my brother was. Through the storm we heard the crack of a rifle shot from somewhere outside, then another and then another.

Carlos returned several minutes later soaking wet. His long black hair glistened with raindrops, his blue work shirt clinging to his muscular physique like a second layer of skin. He was smiling, rifle in hand. "Nicky is dead," he smiled and walked away.

Once the rain stopped, Carlos ordered the ranch hands to dig a deep pit for Nicky in the date grove near the stable. Carlos took a heavy stainless steel chain and wound it around Nicky's still neck. He hitched that chain up to a small tractor and dragged our horse's dead body across the date grove then through the back gate to unceremoniously dump her body into the deep earthen hole, just like he was throwing out the afternoon trash.

My sisters, brother, and I decided that we should have a real funeral service for Nicky. Before the ranch hands could fill in the hole, we marched out of the house in single file, oldest to youngest; I brought up the rear. Gathering around the grave we all cried like little babies. Albert played taps on his coronet. I think I was numb with grief. While Albert played taps, Carlos came up behind me and with his massively strong hands he grabbed me by the back of my belt and lifted me like a yo-yo over the pit where our horse lay dead.

Looking down, I saw Nicky's once smooth neck mauled by the chain. A gaping hole crusted with blood just under Nicky's left ear along with two other bullet holes in her chest drove home the violence of this defenseless animal's death. I screamed out loud, partly from fear tempered with both horror and profound grief, and my sisters and brother were all screaming as well.

The ranch hands laughed nervously out loud as Carlos amused them by first dangling me and then finally dropping me on the ground next to the still open pit. Carlos merely smiled, more of a sneer than a smile; a look of power and control that was inescapable. Nicky's loss was deepened for me by a gut-wrenching realization that the men I trusted so much did not care for me at all. The horror of this realization chilled me to the bone and shook my childhood world.

Carlos was not at all affected by either his wanton act of killing or the grief shared by four children he was charged with watching. No, to the contrary, I believed then and carry that belief forward to this very day that Carlos was simply demonstrating the life or death grip he maintained on our very existence. His grotesque demonstration left an indelible mark on my psyche. The act of cruelty was not only physically painful; it was frightening beyond all understanding for an eight year-old boy.

Albert, Celeste, Anne, and I ran away from the gravesite as fast as we could while Carlos' brothers filled in the grave. Silently retreating to our rooms, we cried until late in the afternoon. Almost as if it were planned, we all emerged around 4:00 PM, deciding to go out to the gravesite with nobody else around. When we got there the site was smoothly covered over; the desert sand dry and uniform in color and texture. There was no indication that Nicky was hidden below.

As usual, Mom was nowhere to be found.

The Answer Man

On one occasion, Mom cast me in the role of a pawn for an adult game. She told me to call my Pop, who was in Chicago, on the phone and ask him if he knew what a bigamist was. My father laughed out loud and said, "Your mom has prepared you very well." Pop meant that mom had briefed me with exactly what to say, as though I was a witness in a courtroom. Then he said that he was very busy and he loved me before he hung up the phone.

When I told Mom what Pop said, she stiffened even more, turned silently around, and walked directly into her bedroom, her place of solace ever since Linda's death. Because I did not understand what had just happened, I asked my brother, Albert, what the word bigamist meant. All Albert said was that Pop had two wives, which both confused and angered me. I didn't understand why Mom's legal expertise couldn't resolve this problem, too.

The Way We Were

During one of his routine visits to the ranch, upon paying Carlos' back wages, my father told Carlos that he was to "discipline the kids". Carlos performed this job with zeal, somehow confusing discipline with additional abuse. He started slapping me in the head even more than before and telling me what a "worthless piece of shit" I was.

Quite often Pop failed to send money to cover the expenses of running the ranch, including money to pay Carlos his salary. While I know this oversight was intended to punish Mom, Carlos only knew he wasn't getting paid; he took it out on all of us with extra special violence. Carlos was beating, humiliating, and sexually abusing my sisters. As the smallest, I was another target of Carlos' relentless and vicious wrath. Even so, as bad as it got, I never gave up. I toughened up as much as any child can, reverted to graveyard humor, and laughed at everything, even when things were seriously bad. My tough resolve only broke down rarely and my internal rage was generally expressed as laughter. Each of our family members developed different strategies to cope with the chaos and the pain.

Albert and Carlos were cut from the same cloth in several ways. Carlos taught Albert to box and to use the light bag so he could beat up other kids when they were picking on him. At one point, Carlos invited the head biker from the Throttle Stompers, a local gang who had been picking on Albert, out to the ranch where Carlos set up a boxing ring as a Saturday afternoon sport. After all, Carlos was a boxer for many years.

Four of Albert's high school buddies and five of the biker gang members were in attendance, plus most of the ranch hands. As usual, I was safely perched up high in the rafters watching the event. Over a three round event, Albert dropped his opponent in each round, earning a great deal of respect from the gang members and ranch hands alike. He ended up developing a friendship with the bikers and never had problems with them again.

Anne and Celeste turned to food for solace when they were 10 and 13 years old. Because of their emotional distress and the fact that our diet was impaired when the money ran scarce, both of my sisters gained a significant amount of weight.

In addition, Celeste became almost mute among the family members. She stopped talking with us as though we didn't exist. Instead of communicating with family members, she focused even more intently on school.

At age 10, Anne was an intimidating girl who asserted herself by picking on me. I retaliated one time by shooting her in the belly with a Daisy air rifle. On this occasion she threated to hit me once again, so I told her, "Take one more step and I will shoot you." She called what she thought was my bluff and stepped forward. I shot her without even realizing how I was stepping into my family patterns. After healing from the bruise, Anne refrained from any other form of aggression toward me. In fact, she appeared to develop a level of trust and respect for my ability to use a gun in the service of self-preservation. That trust would be put to an even more dramatic and potentially lethal test six years later.

When I was not being hit, kicked, punched, or humiliated at home, I was reduced to comforting my mother. Mom emerged periodically from her depressive coma and sometimes climbed into my bed to spend the night with me. Even though it was a king sized bed and there was plenty of room, it never felt right in any way. It wasn't for my benefit that Mom crawled into bed with me. The fact is that I was never comforted or protected by her. This nighttime activity was, in truth, only done for the benefit of Mom alone. The practice continued until I was 10 years old. Perhaps I was Mom's closest connection to my sister, Linda, but there was little if any relationship by this time between Mom and me.

Awakening - Playboy

Albert was in the eighth grade when Carlos brought home a copy of the very first Playboy magazine ever published; Marilyn Monroe was the centerfold. In a classic example of grooming, Carlos shared the controversial magazine with Albert. Later, Albert likewise brought me into the five-room house and showed me where Carlos kept the magazine hidden. I didn't think there was anything nasty about the picture at all. Instead, I was entranced by Monroe's beauty and felt sure I wanted to be with such an exquisite woman.

Previously, I had seen the movie, A Boy and The Dolphin starring Sophia Loren, at the local Aladdin Theater. I was in awe of Sophia's exquisite beauty radiating through her wet gossamer blouse when she climbed into the boat. I didn't know what mystery existed between men and women, but it was perfectly clear to me even at my young age that I wanted to be as close as possible to that gorgeous woman, Sophia Loren.

Circling the Drain

The time eventually came when the Teitelbaum children had to learn to work around the house because so many of the help were being laid off and Pop's financial contributions continued to decline. Albert and I became responsible for outside chores when I was in the third grade. I learned to drive the Ford tractor, water the lawn, cut the grass, edge and trim the rose bushes, fill the cisterns twice a day, disk the grapefruit orchard, irrigate, climb the palm trees, cut the fronds, and forget school work. Unofficially but functionally, I was now a ranch hand, more like a slave than one recognizing the dignity of work, since the work was unpaid.

Celeste and Anne, like maids, cleaned the house, learned to wash clothes, iron, and cook. At first we all did little things, then we ended up working the entire ranch, inside and out, just to keep up appearances.

When the money ran dry, we also had to cut the amount of food we ate. Dog food was not as important as family members' food. I was only allowed to serve 5 cans of dog food for 10 large dogs, even though I knew this was not sufficient. Previously, the dogs were served 15 cans of dog food, 3 to 5 loaves of stale bread, and leftovers from each of our meals on a daily basis.

I watched as the dogs slowly thinned down so much that their ribs and backbones were prominent. I tried to take care of Boy, a large brown Boxer who belonged to Carlos and may have been old anyway. The combination of starvation and old age took the final toll. Eventually, he just lay down. I tried to give him water and a piece of chicken, but he was not interested. I sat down with my back against a palm tree trunk. Boy's chest and head lay across my lap and he passed away in my arms. I was convinced that he starved to death.

Carlos wouldn't even come outside to pay his respects when I told him what happened to his dog. He just made me drag Boy's body out of the yard. I put Boy into my red wagon and took him out to the date grove where I was supposed to bury him deep, which I did. I sat right down where I buried Boy and stayed there under a nearby palm tree. It was very hot, over 100 degrees, but a slight breeze cooled me off. The kid from the next farm came over and sat down with me under that tree. He asked why I had my red wagon in the date groves and I told him I just buried Carlos' dog. He was so frightened about Boy's death, he jumped up and ran back home. Maybe the neighbors knew more about how dangerous Carlos was than I realized.

I just sat hunched over in the grove for a good long time, thinking about this great dog, a fearless, big headed, brown and white Boxer. He liked to play and loved to fight my dog, Rufus. At least 3 times per year it took the whole family to break them up. Sometimes we needed the fire hose to wet them down so we could pull them apart.

It was hard to know what to do about the rest of our dogs, but I did not want them to continue suffering from hunger. When I returned to the kitchen, I took 3 loaves of stale bread from the cupboard, put them in a 5 gallon bucket, added one gallon of water and 10 cans of dog food. Using a big wooden spoon, I mixed up the bread, water, and dog food together, then added leftovers from the refrigerator.

I fed all of the dogs very slowly from this mixture to make sure they all got their share. It took a long time to distribute the meal because they took turns eating. It was almost a ritual event without any fighting between them. It seemed like they knew Boy was gone. They ate all I could give them and drank a lot of water in the afternoon sun on that hot desert day. For about 5 or 6 weeks the dogs were hungry all the time, but on this particular day they had enough to eat.

Later when Carlos came into the kitchen he saw the empty dog food cans, the Webbers bread bags, and figured out what I had done. His next action was very deliberate. He picked me up, covered my face with one hand, and smashed the back of my head into the wall, which collapsed in the shape of my skull. Then he grabbed my arms and smashed my nine-year-old torso into the wall. Again the wall broke under the force. The beating did not stop there; it was only starting. Carlos took off his belt and beat me with it, covering my entire body with painful blows while family members held their breaths and watched from the sidelines. None of the children or adults watching this vicious beating had the courage to intervene on my behalf.

At first I tried to run away and finally stopped trying, but he hit me even more. When I defiantly yelled at him to stop the malicious beating, he hit me with his fist and dropped me to the floor. Even though there had already been many beatings, this was the worst. In my entire life, I never felt closer to death than during this beating. For seven or eight minutes, Carlos tortured me without the slightest pause. I was sure that the end was near, and still feel fortunate to have survived.

The beating occurred on Friday and I was unable to get up or move around until Monday. I had black, blue, and yellow bruises all over my body and stayed in bed for three days. Aunt Hannah brought food into my bedroom. I hurt in places I did not know could hurt, including both of my little feet where Carlos deliberately stomped on and smashed them.

It would have been too dangerous to take me to Dr. Pauley's office. He could not blame this abuse on fencing and would have been required to call the authorities. At least that's what I hope would have happened. However, that was not an option because Dr. Pauley's services were not requested.

Some days afterwards Carlos told me he was sorry and that I had to act responsibly, as we had no money. Then he told me that my father owed him six months pay. That is when I stubbornly reminded Carlos that Boy was his personal dog and that he should have buried him. Carlos responded with couple of slaps to the back of my wounded head. But he knew I was correct.

The next weekend, with bruises covering my entire body, I had to help Carlos patch and paint the holes in the kitchen walls. As defiant as I appeared on the outside, in my head I believed that the beating was completely my fault and I deserved everything Carlos dished out. My family members who failed to protect me were also blameless in the face of my transgressions.

Chapter Nine: 1954

Cloud Burst

On one hot summer day, Carlos, Albert, and I took the Ford tractor to our private garbage dump. Not a cloud was in the sky as we rode up Madison Avenue about one-half mile. Then we turned on our private road and into the date groves to the dumpsite. We unloaded the trailer, dumped the garbage, and lit it on fire. A strong wind came up from out of nowhere and the overhead sky quickly turned dark. We continued to tend the fire until huge raindrops started falling; the thunderclaps were so loud they hurt our ears.

Carlos yelled, "Cloud burst!" He quickly unhooked the trailer from the Ford tractor and started to drive away without regard for our safety. Albert jumped up and dragged me by the wrist over to the tractor with him. We barely made it safely onto the moving tractor and my heart was pounding; I knew that if Albert's grip failed, my fate would certainly be to fall beneath the tractor wheels, especially because of Carlos' erratic driving. Carlos drove as fast as he could push that old tractor while the rain came down so hard, it stung. Even though I could not see where we were, we made it back from the garbage dump to the pavement on Madison Avenue. We continued west towards the compound, passed by the main gates, and headed into the date grove. With tractor wheels throwing water and mud higher than its passengers; we must have looked like a speedboat.

We came to a quick stop by the side gate and ran into the kitchen, soaked and muddy from head to foot. First we cleaned up ourselves only to spend even more time cleaning up the mud we tracked into our otherwise spotless kitchen. There were still elements of excitement, danger, and exhilaration coursing through my veins.

Donuts in the Living Room

Times were tough; we looked for fun wherever we could find it, doing anything we could to blow off steam in an oppressive environment. A few years before the financial door closed, my father gifted us with two beautiful red, battery-powered, miniature Jeeps. Four children could be seated at the same time in each Jeep, even though they were smaller than golf carts. They had been kept in one of the garages against the wall, completely covered with gray canvas tarps since 1948.

One Friday night when Carlos was away from home, Albert uncovered both Jeeps and began charging them. By Saturday morning, the four Teitelbaum children joined forces and washed down the miniature Jeeps until they sparkled like new again. We tested them out by racing around the yard, following a series of concrete paths. When we tired of the paved path routes, we opened up the double doors into our main living room and raced in circles around the furniture. After breaking a lamp, spilling battery acid, and leaving tire tracks indoors, we exited the living room and made donuts in the lawn outside.

Carlos arrived back at the ranch just in time to catch us doing donuts on his precious lawn. Every single one of us was thrashed, pummeled, whipped, and sent to our rooms without any supper. As frightening as that might sound to an outsider, it was just more of the same for us and well worth the pleasure of the moment; if we hadn't been beaten for playing with the Jeeps, we would have been beaten for something else not nearly as interesting and perhaps not even our fault. At least we could claim ownership for this event.

The next day Carlos loaded the Jeeps on the bed of our pickup truck and took them away. When he returned with six bags of groceries, it was clear that he made a some kind of profit. Many years later it was discovered that Carlos actually sold only one of the Jeeps and stored the other one at his parents' house. We finally learned about this when the second Jeep emerged from storage upon Carlos' eventual move from Indio to Los Angeles.

Spilling the Beans

During that same time, Pop became an attractive target for mobsters who wanted a piece of his political and financial power. Thanks to a police surveillance microphone planted in Jimmy Weinberg's office in 1954, two hit men were overheard planning to toss Pop out his office window on tenth floor, with the intention to make it look like a suicide. Since Pop was already experiencing tax problems, there might have been some acceptable rationale for suicide.

Upon overhearing the plans to murder my father, police rushed in to put twenty-four hour police bodyguards on him. The hit details were revealed to Pop, including the potential perpetrators' names: 'Needle Nose' Labriola and Jimmy Weinberg. Their goal had been to take over the Chicago Restaurant Union where Pop served as Chief Council. However, they could not gain control of the lucrative business while Pop was still alive. Their greed cost them their lives; in a couple of months both Labriola and Weinberg were found dead in the trunk of a car next to the Chicago River. They had first been poisoned, then strangled, and finally shot before being packed in the trunk.

The local newspaper implied that the attempt to kill Pop without the permission of the mob was a sin to the outfit, which probably led to Weinberg and Labriola's murder. Police also spread the rumor that Weinberg and Labriola were trading information from the mob to the police and vice versa. That act of treachery further sealed their fate. I suppose in comparison, our childhood traumas were less compelling to Pop. He had bigger fish to fry.

Aquatic Man

Albert was a first-class diver and a champion swimmer at Coachella Valley Union High School (CVUHS). By 1952, he was swimming up to fifty laps daily in our pool. He turned into a swimming machine during races and became almost unbeatable. He was a regular at the swimming meets, received countless blue ribbons, and had a bevy of girlfriends closely following his progress.

After the bathroom conflict, Albert's mean streak toward me grew in a particular form of retribution. Whenever he snapped his fingers I was supposed to obey his demands like a dog. He frequently insisted that I spot him in the pool when he did laps.

One day I finished swimming ten laps and was pretty well worn out. Albert yelled, "Hey, dumb shit," and told me to spot him as he did a racing spin at the far end of the pool. He wanted me to stand on a particular spot to show how close he was to the far end of the pool, a distance that gave him just enough room to perform a precise spin-turn without crashing into the wall.

As instructed, I took four giant steps away from the end of the pool and stood on the intended mark. When Albert started his lap, though, I took 2 giant steps back toward the end of the pool so that he would not have sufficient notice to begin his turn. The subsequent impact of his face on the pool tile was harsh and dramatic, causing serious damage to Albert's face.

After his broken nose was set and healed, Albert looked much better. There was something about that event that evened the playing field just a little bit, and seemed to increase Albert's respect for me either despite or because of his wounds. Whatever the case, his bossiness decreased to a more tolerable level. Just like the Daisy air rifle incident with Anne, I had further developed and been rewarded for 'family' style survival skills.

Ranch House Traitors

Carlos' family lived about two miles away, next to the All American Canal. His father and mother had twenty children, the youngest was four years old and still others were older than Carlos. Unfortunately, a major fire completely destroyed their family home, which was situated among many other previously abandoned houses, all occupied at that time by transient families. Since my father owed Carlos back wages, it appeared that Carlos decided to host a 'fire sale' at the Teitelbaum house.

I was about 11 years old when Carlos awakened me late at night. He told me to stay quiet and remain in bed regardless of what happened. Four of our ranch workers entered my room, opened my bedroom closet, and helped themselves to over half of its contents. They pillaged my toys and the Golden Books I had been reading since I was two years old. They took most of my clothes, including my favorite red fireman pajamas with feet. Their next stop was my sisters' room where they did the same.

After they picked through our bedrooms, Ann and Celeste watched them clean the ranch of various pieces of furniture, dishes, silverware, and other household items. The kitchen was entirely emptied of food. The only areas they did not enter were my mother's wing of the house and the section where Albert's, Carlos', and Hannah's bedrooms were located.

The next day at Herbert Hoover School, we saw Carlos' younger siblings dressed up in our own clothes, likely brown bagging our food. They had been our playmates for many years but in my mind this was an intolerable betrayal. I was beyond angry; I stopped talking to them, although I knew even then that it wasn't their fault.

The books that I never saw again had been my main treasure. They were connected to sweet memories with Aunt Hannah, who taught me to read from them. A night had not passed without me reading one or another of those books. There were stories of adventure and inspiration. Treasure Island, Moby Dick, and all of the beautiful Golden Books were taken away on that horrifying night. Of the many items that were stolen, those were the most important to me and the most missed.

I was particularly surprised that Carlos' family members took our sweaters and jackets, as summer was coming. Who needed sweaters and jackets in Indio before summer? They were probably good for earning a few dollars at a yard sale, though.

It felt like pirates and thugs raided us, except that we knew the thieves very well. My sisters were devastated that their Raggedy Ann and Raggedy Andy dolls were stolen. They also had over twenty porcelain dolls, but for some reason, none of those were taken. Luckily, the ball of chewed gum that my sister Celeste had been collecting over the years was not stolen and remained in its esteemed place on her bookshelf.

A couple of sizeable items were also taken from the five-room house. One was a very large, steel, self-propelled, merry-go-round made in Chicago, which seated four, and the other was a large carnival sized roller coaster on tracks. Assembling and disassembling this equipment was onerous enough that they were used only periodically, perhaps four times per year for special events.

Mom appeared to be unhappy, but not outraged, about what had been done in the midnight raid and she confronted Carlos about it in our presence. Her reaction, however, was extremely confusing and disorienting to me. Instead of anger, Mom simply explained to Carlos that he should have asked for permission to take what he did and insisted that she should have been able to choose what was stolen from her house. I didn't understand how Mom could ask to choose what was stolen. Carlos self-righteously said that he had not been paid in 3 months and Mom responded that $1,800 was not a reason to take a full house of clothing, furniture, and books.

Mom asked Carlos, "What did you take from your own room?" Carlos replied, "Nothing." Mom indignantly pointed her finger at him and said, "Remember that this is a lesson. Now get into your room and take what your family needs." His closet was filled with suits and jeans, which his brothers could have used, but I don't know if Carlos followed through with Mom's demand.

Several days after the burglary, an insurance assessor walked through the house with my mother, recording all of the losses in a notebook. Six weeks later, he returned with papers for Mom's signature and gave her an envelope with a settlement check. Carlos drove Mom and me to the Bank of America so Mom could deposit some of the money and pick up a cashier's check for the balance, which she immediately mailed to Pop in Chicago.

It was just a couple of years later during Pop's IRS hearings for tax fraud when his additional claim of a $50,000 burglary loss was denied because there was evidence that the loss had already been paid by the insurance company. Mom's absence during the theft and her very unusual response to Carlos, along with the significant insurance compensation that was divided between Mom and Pop, and Pop's subsequent claim about a $50,000 loss all mark the theft as having been an elaborate plan, whether it had been developed before or after the Martén's house fire. The material sacrifices, however, paled in comparison to the traumatic impact of this ill-conceived act on all of the Teitelbaum children.

Machismo

By this time, Carlos and Hannah were living together in the room where Linda died. I hated that Carlos and Hannah were a couple because he had no respect for women and I loved her. I would rather have seen her with Benjamin Siegel, who showed more respect than Carlos ever could. Carlos was beneath her and it was beyond me how Hannah could have been attracted to him.

Carlos was not only the most vicious pedophile I could ever imagine, he was also the most self-absorbed, narcissistic and vile person I could ever conger up. He spent untold hours working his punching bags, lifting weights, measuring his biceps, and admiring himself in front of the mirror. He was concerned about his clothing, wearing nothing but well pressed suits and fancy shoes. Unfortunately, one of Carlos' favorite punching bags was Aunt Hannah.

Pop came to the ranch about two months after the theft and stayed four days. He paid Carlos what was owed him and gave Mom an envelope, nothing even close to a hat-box. There was just enough money to cover our debts and immediate expenses for six additional months and not a cent more.

Pop did not have many visitors on this trip, so we had plenty of time with him. As always, he spent most of his time in the library and also in the bedroom with Mom. It seemed like this was a relaxing visit for Pop, who could fall sleep anywhere, in a chair, in the car, or even in a courtroom. Even though he had a mild case of narcolepsy, he always awoke fully oriented to the exact moment when he drifted off without ever missing a beat.

Guardian Angel

Clemie Johnson, a big loving woman, was our night maid for about 5 years beginning in 1949. She was a very large woman of African American descent with an angelic personality who cared deeply for my sisters and me, watching over us during her work schedule, which included Monday through Friday nights. Just like a shepherd sleeping near a gate, Clemie slept on the floor outside of my bedroom door so that nobody could enter uninvited during the night. Since Carlos' midnight raid occurred on a Saturday night, Clemie was not there to protect us.

When Pop cut financial support again in 1954, we had to let Clemie Johnson go. She stayed one extra week and never asked for any money, as she was "concerned to the safety" of me and my siblings, whom she called her "children". She was well loved by every one of us. Never again did we feel so completely loved or protected by any one person.

Mom also let other cooks and maids go, since we could not pay them anymore. The butler and most of the ranch hands were let go several months before, so Clemie was the last to leave. It may have been one of Mom's nicest acts, keeping a place for Clemie with us as long as possible in spite of our rapidly declining resources. Of course, all of the abandoned responsibilities were reassigned to the children who remained in residence at the Loveless Ranch.

Working in the Sun

My after school jobs on Mondays and Thursdays were to mow the front lawn between the big house and the pool, carry buckets of water to the 30 rose bushes that lined the walkways on both sides of the yard next to the eleven foot high walls, edge the lawn, carry the grass cuttings in a wheelbarrow to the outside the wall near the date gardens, then add chlorine to the pool and refill it if necessary. When the chores were completed it was time for dinner and some television, then I went off to bed.

Every Tuesday and Friday my work included cutting the grass around the tennis courts, weeding and hoeing around the flower gardens, carrying water in buckets to the roses, and pulling weeds with my bare hands. Carlos prohibited our use of gloves so at least once a week our hands would bleed after doing chores. Lava Soap was the only thing that could get our hands anywhere near clean, but it was pretty painful to use after pulling weeds because of the open wounds. Later in the day I picked grapefruits and oranges, then washed down the tennis courts and tightened up the tennis court's net ropes.

On Wednesdays, Saturdays, and Sundays, it was my job to load the trailer with eight large garbage cans and take garbage from the big house, rumpus room, and the five-room house to our private dump among the tall date trees on the back ten acres. Then I drove the tractor to the end of the property where our farm workers lived. I got in trouble at least a dozen times for driving the tractor through the town of Indio, irritating the police chief who called my Mom to tell her I was driving through town yet again. After cruising downtown Indio in a muddy tractor, I visited Maria, Carlos' sister, who rewarded me with fresh, delicious tacos. She sizzled them in grease until they were sizzling hot, crispy, and mouth-watering.

Later in the evening I rode the tractor and trailer back to the compound, filled it with gas, and stored it outside the big wall near the gas tank. By then darkness was setting in, so I washed up for dinner. When I was already full of Maria's tacos, I was chastised for not eating at the dinner table. By simply moving my plate a few inches forward, a signal went up to everyone at the table that no defensive forking maneuvers would be employed that day and my siblings were free to graze without danger.

Turn the Radio On

It seemed like a miracle that our eight foot Steinway remained in the living room despite Carlos' apparent pillaging. When Mom was feeling all right and could come out of her bedroom, she played tunes made popular during her lifetime. She was adept at reading music and picked up contemporary songs easily. It made Mom especially happy when we sang along with her and it usually sounded as though we knew what we were doing.

One morning just before Christmas, Mom and I went to perform at the KREO AM radio station in Indio, which Mom arranged for me because my voice was pure and its pitch was still in the upper registers. I sang, "I Saw Mommy Kissing Santa Claus," while Mom provided the piano accompaniment without regard to our Jewish heritage.

Afterwards, I was driven back to Herbert Hoover Middle School to finish out the day. I was unaware of the fact that the school transmitted the entire radio show over the public announcement speakers, and took a lot of razzing from jealous classmates. It didn't hurt my feelings at all that I had distinguished myself as a radio performer.

A Bad Break

One day when Pop arrived at the ranch, I fell off the jungle gym high bar at school during recess. I broke my right forearm, which meant yet another trip to Dr. Pauley's office. He just shook his head and then said, "Robert, this is going to hurt." He was absolutely right. It hurt something terrible when he set it and wrapped up my arm in a cast. Afterwards, he took an x-ray to make sure it was in place and then sent me home.

This should have been a fairly isolated and typical childhood injury. Instead, my early years were riddled with unreported, untreated injuries, which would have revealed serious, ongoing, neglect and abuse from my caregivers and parents if the resulting injuries were diagnosed and treated properly. As it turned out, legions of abuses went into the 'family secrets' repository; to this day I am unaware of those injuries' long-term after effects.

Carrillo's Heaven

During the good times, the family piled into the limo driven by Carlos to have dinner at Rancho Carrillo. Not quite a restaurant, rather it was a private home on Madison and 48th, where we were treated to a family style sit-down meal with all the guests gathered around one large banquet table. The grandmother of the house cooked for no more than ten to fifteen people each Saturday evening and the authentic Mexican food she served was heavenly. The host family was very friendly and their children were frequent playmates for us even though there was a great language divide. Carlos joined the host family for dinner while we all ate at the banquet table. I consider it to be a great gift that we were able to enjoy these simple pleasures with others despite the embodied danger in a nearby room.

Virtual Mother

Things were not going very well in 1955 but we were managing the best we could. I often sat in the living room next to my mother's bedroom and listened to car races on the elegant large vacuum-tube radio. It was during one of those radio shows that I remember hearing about Bill Vukovich's death. He was my favorite driver, having won the Indy 500 in 1953 and 1954. When he was killed in 1955, I stopped listening to car races completely.

Instead, I started watching wrestling and boxing on the big TV. When there was a boxing match, I knocked at Mom's door and let her know who was fighting. If the match included someone she liked, she came out and sat with her arms around me to watch, an homage to her younger years as Kid Melnick. This may have been the most normal family style activity the two of us ever shared; it was certainly a very small slice of my young life. I accepted that this was all I could have with her and relished the moments.

Crushing Accident

I was nine years old, riding on my brother's racing bike in the early afternoon of August 1. Two of Carlos' younger sisters joined me on borrowed family bikes. It was Saturday and we were riding in the outer compound near the five-room house and the garages. The front gate was open so I decided to exit through the gate, make a sharp U-turn in the driveway, and return back to the compound through the same opening.

Because of my speed, I missed the driveway turn and rode straight out into the street. It was too late to avoid the approaching car. Immediately upon impact, the handle bar pierced my upper leg and then I was tossed up into the air. Everything started moving in slow motion. I hit the left front windshield of a 1955 Buick Roadmaster, right in front of a frantic woman's face. I saw and heard her scream as my body first busted the window, then was pitched back up into the air before finally slamming down onto the pavement. I rolled to a stop with my face flat on the asphalt, looking toward the front gate. I could not move at all but was not in any pain.

In a stupor, I recognized family and strangers rushing toward me. Aunt Hannah picked me up off the pavement and first carried me into the house, then back outside into a car for a trip to Dr. Pauley's office, where I was immediately transported into surgery.

I had an out of body experience during surgery. It felt like I was watching the entire event from above the operating room lights. I could see the nurses and doctors preparing my leg, cleaning out the massive wound of debris and shredded blue jeans, irrigating the blood, and bandaging my leg and face. I lost large patches of skin and observed the medical activities from the out of body vantage point as the surgical team completed their work and stitched me up.

In another flash I was back on the table and Dr. Pauley was right there in front of my face. Immediately, I told him what I had seen. He said that I was blessed and explained that my experience was an effect of the anesthesia, like a dream. He wrote down everything I told him, which made me think it was important.

The strange part of the entire experience was that I really had no pain. It must have been a great shock to my body. After going home from the hospital, however, I could hardly walk and was bedridden for a few days. I finally got up and limped into the bathroom where there was a bench with two stairs. I climbed up in front of the bathroom mirror. My face was banged up and scabs covered the right side of my head and all the way down to my chin and neck.

While standing in front of the mirror I looked past the wounds and into my eyes. It struck me that I was really alive and I could see something about both my past and my future in my eyes. I had been hurt, attacked, and abused many times over the past years and could still stand. The future, as it was revealed in my eyes, confirmed that no matter what happened or was yet to happen, I would always get up with the ability to look adversity straight in the eye; it was clear in that moment that my future didn't have to be defined by my past.

After four weeks, I returned to Dr. Pauley for a follow-up check. By now there was significant pain in my leg, which was growing steadily worse. He opened up the wound and pulled out a one-inch piece of Levi's jeans and a couple of gravel sized rocks, then cleansed and reclosed the wound. Dr. Pauley asked me to tell him about my experience in the operating room once more. He wrote everything down a second time; it must have really been important.

I also told him about looking into the bathroom mirror, seeing the past and the future in my own eyes. He took notes about that experience, as well. In his own way, Dr. Pauley was affirming me. He explained that looking into your own eyes was a form of reflective meditation and that when you look into your own soul and ask yourself questions, you cannot lie.

I finally healed well after this appointment. There was a little more time off from school to recover, but when I was better Carlos gave me another beating for being on Albert's bike and for not avoiding the car. He was determined to regain what he knew was his rightful role as my primary tormentor; he would not allow life's random tragedies to surpass his own evil intentions to break me down. To Carlos, my value was less than spit.

On my first day back in school, I climbed out of the limo and saw a large group of children run toward me. They were chanting, "Teitelbaum is back, Teitelbaum is back." It surprised and overjoyed me to realize that anybody cared. Even though Carlos was present, since he drove me to school, I understood, at least for the moment, that not everyone wanted to destroy me. My friends, Johnnie, Teddy, and Richard lifted me up, hugged me, and helped me to class.

Although I still had trouble walking after returning to school, I tried to get back into a learning state of mind. That definitely didn't last very long. My work schedule at home grew quickly and there was no time to study before dark. After dinner I retreated to my room and usually fell right to sleep from exhaustion.

This was another year of continuous beatings. Sometimes when I mowed the lawn, Carlos threw a rock at me, hitting me in the back. If I sat at the table for a meal, he slapped the back of my head. He continually called me a worthless piece of shit. This sadistic activity simply became normal for me; everyone must live like this, I thought, since everyone at the Loveless Ranch was a target for Carlos' abuse.

Knock-Out Radio Show

There were usually eight people or more at breakfast and getting everyone together at the same time was no easy feat. Celeste had a small portable radio, which she and Anne listened to in their bedroom each morning while getting ready for the day. They shut it off just before running to the breakfast table for a family meal.

One morning Carlos walked into the kitchen with Celeste's radio in hand and plugged it in near the third stove. Celeste said, "That is my radio," and Carlos replied, "You do not get ready on time and we have to wait for you, so now it stays in the kitchen." Celeste again protested, saying that it was her birthday gift. Carlos' face turned ugly, reflecting the rage he internalized over the years, and he responded to Celeste's protests by yelling, "I am in charge!" He jumped up, grabbed the radio, held it up in front of us, then turned away. Like a baseball pitcher, he wound up his arm and deliberately smashed the radio into the marble kitchen floor, destroying it completely.

He began ranting that we were all going to pay for not doing everything he demanded immediately, the very moment he barked out an order. Aunt Hannah stood up from the kitchen table, faced him, and threw her cup of coffee right in his face. She yelled at him, insisting that he did not have the right to talk to any of the children that way. He grabbed her by the neck and choked her, then hit her with a quick punch to the face. The force was so hard that we all heard a crack. Aunt Hannah instantly hit the floor like a rag doll and did not move for over fifteen minutes. By now we were all screaming, including cousin Claudia.

All eight of us at the table were scared that Carlos killed Aunt Hannah. When she finally started moving again, we helped her into her room, the same room where Linda died in 1948. It was just down the hall from the kitchen. Aunt Hannah's face turned black and blue right away. She recovered but the black, blue, and green bruises on her face took a very long time to disappear.

Everyone knew that Carlos was sinister and we also knew that he was in charge of my siblings, aunts, mother, me, and anyone else who graced our doorstep. We had already been walking on eggshells around him for several years. Now we were also frightened about how easily and quickly he could destroy the people we loved. He broke Aunt Hannah down in the same way that he broke each of us. My love for her never diminished, but the safety I felt in her arms since birth died on this disturbingly dangerous day. The haunting memories of that horrible event continue to grip every one of us.

Chapter Eleven: 1956 – 1957

Reciprocity Denied

It was very hard for me to accept that Pop also had a home at 609 Hillcrest in Beverly Hills with Roxanne and their four children. Every time I thought about it, I felt angry and betrayed by Pop. Then he came home again in 1956, larger than life in a white suit and a big white hat. He had put on even more weight and was probably up to 325 pounds at 5'11" tall. I always figured that I would grow up to be larger than life, too.

Pop's visit was not intended as a social call. Rather, he asked Mom to research a paper for him because he knew that he was going to be indicted again for income tax evasion. Pop worked with Mom in the library for four days, developing a strategy to protect him from the tax courts that were hounding him. Mom's research saved the day yet again so that Pop was able to "call off the dogs" for a while. He wasn't indicted for anything else until three years later. I knew Pop was pleased because he stayed with us longer than he had originally intended. He was teaching me how he rewarded people who supported him by gracing them with his presence, and how a man's obligation ended there. Out of sight, out of mind.

Since Pop reached out to Mom for help, I figured this was also my chance to ask for his support. I told him that Carlos had been hitting me on a regular basis. His response was that I should toughen up, and he talked about how difficult it was for him growing up in Brooklyn. He reminded me that life is rough, and described how he depended on his big sister Ilana to protect him. Then he summarily changed the topic and repeated the story about Nicky pulling me out of the pool in Chicago in order to cheer me up.

Maybe as an attempt to offer me an incentive, he told me how great things were for him during this time in his life. Even if that was true for him, things were the pits for his first family; my efforts to find some help from my father failed miserably. More than anything, what I learned on this day was that I could not count on Pop for support or protection. I also learned through his example to help others whenever I could but only when it was in my own interest; even to the detriment of my own family.

I never understood why Mom and Pop slept together when he was visiting the ranch. Everyone, including kids in the first family, knew that Mom and Pop's marriage had ended. It struck me that Pop had a second family whom he betrayed with his first family. Even though he had no boundaries, his transgression against the second family during the current visit lit a spark of hope within me that maybe he was coming home to stay where I thought he belonged.

Before Pop left, he gave Mom the traditional envelope that helped us get through another year. He might just as well have left the envelope on the bureau in payment for services rendered, like he had done with so many other women. Pop returned to his second family with his suit perfect, a smile on his face, and no booze on his breath.

Like always, the first thing Mom did with the money Pop left was to pay Carlos what he was owed. It seemed obvious to everyone that Mom favored Carlos in ways that I cannot even bear to imagine or even discuss. She also paid all of the other town members who carried our debts, and for a short time things were calm again. Even amidst the calm, by the time the limo pulled away with Pop in it, my passionate yet fragile dreams of reconstructing our family as a unit had completely dissolved.

Eventually, Pop was indicted for income tax evasion. However, because of the work Mom and Pop did during this particular visit, Pop's lifestyle was not affected for several years and the Federal Tax Court stopped hounding him at least temporarily. Even as a young boy, I knew that a cloud of danger followed our family because of the tax problems and assumed that we may someday be homeless. All we could do in the meantime was distract ourselves with admittedly dangerous pastimes.

Suicide Shift

Albert talked to Mom when he was 17 years old to see whether he could have a motorcycle. The independence a motorcycle offered would have released him from some of Carlos' scrutiny. It took financial contributions from Pop, but Albert finally got a Harley-Davidson with a suicide shift, which is located by the engine block rather than the handlebars. It's called a suicide shift because the driver must remove one hand from the handlebars in order to shift. One of Albert's friends, Buford, came over to teach him how to ride it. They took off together and six hours later we got 'the call' that everyone dreads, informing us that both of them were in the hospital.

Buford was two times wider than Albert and just got banged up, probably because of his extra padding. Albert was badly but not mortally wounded. The brake handle was pushed through his right hand and he was bruised from head to foot. They sewed Albert's hand back together and sent him home. When the motorcycle was fixed and polished again, it sold for $200 more than what Mom paid for it, which delighted her.

Albert convalesced on the big yellow couch in the living room for about a week. When any one of his three girl friends came over to comfort him, there were many opportunities for each one of them to give Albert some personal attention. The rose gardens were in full bloom, there were plenty of discreet places for them to meet, and the pool's rumpus room was set up like a boarding house. This level of promiscuity, an inheritance from our father, had already become an enduring lifestyle pattern for Albert.

Selective Hearing

Mom called Pop in Beverly Hills and begged him for money as we were again in desperate need of basic support. Finally he agreed that he would help Mom if she would sign away her ownership rights on the property, move out within a year, and continue to help him with legal problems as needed. After she agreed, he called Uncle Michael, his brother, who still lived in the nearby Palm Springs house, asking Michael to bring us some much needed food. Three weeks later Uncle Michael and some of his children pulled up in a new station wagon, and the back was filled with big brown bags. Each grocery bag was overflowing with canned food, eggs, milk, and other staples. One of my young cousins standing at the back of the car asked Uncle Michael, "Why do we have to give these people any food?" He made it sound as though we were strangers.

There was enough food delivered in Uncle Michael's station wagon to last through the entire month. He also brought papers for Mom to sign and an envelope with enough money to pay off the electric company, grocery stores, and others who carried our current debts.

I was glad to see Uncle Michael, even under the circumstances. He was a stranger to us for many years, since about 1951. Before that time, Uncle Michael liked to join us in the swimming pool, where he delighted in holding people under water until they were half-way done in, and then he pulled them up quickly and laughed out loud. Uncle Michael and Aunt Ilana maintained allegiance to my Pop throughout the years, since he continued to hold the purse strings for all of them.

Aunt Ilana moved in with Uncle Michael following her divorce from the Count. She helped care for Michael's children because she didn't have children of her own, and they all developed strong, warm relationships that lasted a lifetime. Even though it was sad that we did not get to grow up together, it is fortunate that they escaped the cruelties we endured.

Friend and Foe

During sixth grade I took another severe beating from Carlos while I was already being punished for not watering the roses enough. The first punishment prohibited me from using the hose. Instead, as an eleven year old boy weighing 80 pounds, I was forced to carry five gallon buckets of water, each weighing half my body weight, the length of a football field each way, sixty times, to deliver two buckets of water for each of the thirty rose bushes. Carlos said that I spilled too much water while carrying the buckets, so for a second punishment, he hit me with his fist, threw rocks at me, and finished the beating off by using the four-foot horsewhip on me. Blood was dripping from my back and legs through all of my clothes. Carlos washed me off with peroxide and water in my mother's bathroom, and then he told me to say nothing, or he would do even worse.

The next day when I went to school, my friend, Johnny, saw blood on the back of my shirt and pants and he quickly ran to tell my homeroom teacher. The teacher quietly examined my wounds and in a shaky yet controlled voice asked me what happened. I told him that I was punished because I did not carry enough water to the rose bushes, and that if I had done a better job I would not have been beaten.

After closing his eyes and taking several deep breaths, my teacher accompanied me to the principal's office and repeated my story to him. The two of them examined me together without uttering another word, although it was clear from the look on their faces and their exchanged glances that they were horrified. It's hard to say whether they were more frightened from seeing my wounds or from imagining the danger they might incur if they actually reported the abuse.

Ultimately, the principal drove me home and dropped me off at the front gate, but he did not even attempt to come through the gates to the front door of our house. The intimidation he felt from our family's reputation meant there would be no legally mandated phone calls or reports. Neither the principal nor my teacher did anything to help me in that situation or in any situation at all.

Nothing changed except that my homeroom teacher resigned from teaching during the very same year and moved to Los Angeles where he took a job as a personal trainer on Wilshire in the Fairfax District. He revealed to me years later that my abuse broke his heart and destroyed his belief that he was competent to protect his students. He couldn't pretend to uphold a teacher's responsibility because of those circumstances. There were a few allies in the community, but their stakes were low. We could only watch out for ourselves. Unfortunately, our self-defense skills were usually short lived and ineffective.

Hand to Mouth

Mom had some very good friends in Indio, so when we did not get money from Pop we went to see the butcher and his wife at the Meat Market. The butcher gave us a tab and allowed us to pay it back when we could. We cut way back on milk and drank powdered milk or water instead. Kool Aid took the place of soda. Meals were routinely limited to the basics such as eggs, white bread, beans, rice, cereal, and chicken. Carlos sometimes gifted us with a goat head, which we roasted and then split open with a hammer to serve goat brains. Even though I loved lamb, goat head was so disgusting that I could not even touch it. All of the Teitelbaum children brought brown bag lunches to school but none ever contained any goat head.

Shields' Date Gardens was the number one produce packing company in the valley. Our workers picked the dates, grapefruit, and oranges from the ranch's eight acres and filled wooden lugs for Shields. Mom used the money to pay tabs that we owed, and we were able to cover basic expenses this way.

Sometimes I took my red wagon into the groves before the workers went through, picked oranges and pink grapefruit, and boxed them up in wooden crates. When I delivered those boxes to tourists staying at the motel next door, I earned $1.50 per lug. The total earnings amounted to $15.00 on a typical Saturday, with $14.75 going to Mom for groceries and twenty-five cents left over for me. Mom never asked how I came by the money and was oblivious to the oddly consistent amount, but she was always very pleased to receive her share. She never acknowledged or applauded my initiative. It was as though she expected me to take care of her and I was pleased to serve in that role when nobody else would.

I was pretty proud of myself as a wage earner and finally regained a sense of worth for contributing to the family. At age twelve, I had stepped up a little bit as a family provider. With my twenty-five cent cut, I spent ten cents at Sniff's Date Garden Café for a Coke and a 7-Up, which I mixed together in a glass of ice, and I still had fifteen cents left over. Those were delicious, satisfying, and happy moments for me.

About three months later Carlos found out about my business venture. He beat me into the ground and told me to never sell any citrus from our ranch. Later on I found out from Fred, Carlos' brother, that Carlos was getting twenty-five cents kickback per lug from the farmworkers he hired to pick our citrus fruit. Once again, someone was infringing on his territory, and this time that someone was me. I had been cutting into his profit. My newly reclaimed sense of worth, which had been tied to self-initiative and hard work, was quickly undone.

This was the first time I remember considering that working for my father might be a worthwhile alternative. If I was a gangster like him, I believed that I would have plenty of money, there would be food in the refrigerator, and most importantly, I could help my mother and sisters escape Carlos' torment and cruelty. In retrospect, while both of my sisters would have welcomed this escape, there is no indication whatsoever that Mom wanted to be separated from Carlos.

The Fifth Amendment

Celeste continued to hold the family title of resident scholar. Her academic coping skills were exemplary. Even when things were the worst at home, she completed all of her school assignments and was at the top of her class. During the summer of 1956, at age fifteen, she attended an enrichment summer session in Northwestern University in Evanston, Illinois, to study forensics. Celeste was excited to escape our terrible environment and I was happy for her, and even though I missed her, watching her leave somehow gave me a little hope that one day I would be as lucky.

When she arrived in Illinois, Pop was on television and in the papers, testifying in front of the McClellan Racketeering Committee. During that hearing, Pop repeatedly invoked the fifth amendment, which made Robert Kennedy livid. Pop called Robert Kennedy very harsh names and criticized their family's road to wealth through Joe Senior's bootlegging activities. Here he was, my paternal 'pot' calling the Kennedy 'kettle' black.

All of the derogatory hearing details were spelled out in Chicago newspapers. On top of everything that happened at home, all the years of abuse, chaos, and fear, the Chicago publicity about Pop pushed Celeste over the edge. She had a nervous breakdown and was sent back home on an airplane. Modeling after Mom's coping style, Celeste stayed in her bedroom for a couple of months and comforted herself by reading. It was as though her ultimate hope for peace was completely shattered and she retreated to her cave.

Over time the Loveless Ranch generated two very different coping skills, depression and acting out. Anne chose the latter path; she ran away from home when she was thirteen years old and remained missing for two days. I was in the car when we finally found her aimlessly walking the streets in Indio. She told me she could not handle being at the house anymore. Her anger upon being returned to that abusive home was evident to everyone, even though she apparently couldn't tolerate street life either. Today I wonder why those were her only two options.

Mom finally asked local politician friends to persuade the newspapers to stop reporting on Pop's troubles in order to protect the children. Out of respect, the Coachella Valley Press omitted future references to the Racketeering Committee events. Even so, other sources for those stories included Life and the L.A. Herald Examiner. It seemed, once again, that there was no escape.

Duck and Cover

My seventh grade homeroom teacher, Mrs. Gibbs, knew that I was studying for my Bar Mitzvah with my grandfather twice each month on Sundays in Beverly Hills. I am sure her intentions were good when Mrs. Gibbs asked me to talk to the class about being Jewish. I was surprised and happy that I could finally share some of my family heritage, in contrast to fitting in with others' religious traditions. For many years, I had literally been singing in the Christmas choirs.

I worked hard at developing a presentation for them and one Friday, four weeks after the invitation, wearing my Yarmulke and Tallis, I told all of the homeroom students the story of Passover from the Haggadah, the great story from the five books of Moses, including the exodus of the Jewish people. I was as proud as anybody could be, and my tolerant friends were supportive and appreciative. However, when I left class that day, other kids cursed me for being a Christ killer and called me a Jew boy. After opening up some of my personal life to everyone, I was roundly rejected by the bigots among my peers. The mental and emotional beatings I experienced at school felt just like home to me. I had not yet developed the capacity to discern friend from foe. As in the childhood game, Mother May I, this event forced me to take three giant steps forward into the legacy of my father's corrupt world.

My science teacher at the same school, a grumpy, opinionated older man, who never said my name correctly, told the class on the day after my presentation that the Jews really had killed Christ. He also told them that the stories I shared in Mrs. Gibbs' class were all lies. His insults were the last straw for me. I finally gave up completely on school. I could not think in class and definitely could not concentrate on any schoolwork at home. My behavior took a serious downward spiral. Three giant, spiral steps downward. Two other friends in abusive families joined together with me to wreck as much havoc at school as we could.

The school officials eventually sent parent monitors into class to see for themselves how disruptive we were, even in front of visitors. I liked to teach kids in class how to make match guns from clothespins, show them how to use a straw to hurl spitballs, and challenge them to Indian wrestling. Albert taught me a new and enjoyable wrestling trick, scissoring my legs around classmates' bodies and squeezing them into submission. My destructive momentum was increasing at a rapid pace during seventh grade.

Acting out did me no good in the long run since nobody understood why I was doing it. Even the children's parents were frightened that my parents would call some bad guy to rough them up, so I was neither counseled nor disciplined. They had no idea that I was acting out to generate enough attention so my sisters and I could be released from the Loveless Ranch concentration camp. There were no Cossacks intimidating my ancestors anymore, merely the overbearing presence of Carlos who endangered us; abuse had become chillingly systemic. Abuse was pervasive within my family and was destroying every remaining thread of integrity.

Throughout this period, I kept studying Hebrew with my grandfather Herman twice a month in Los Angeles. I loved his company, especially during the tumultuous times. He was kind, religious, and devoted to me. My greatest hope was that we could continue working together for a very long time. Like so many other of my dreams, it was not to be so.

Chapter Twelve: 1958

Just Pull the Trigger

In June, 1958, Anne finally revealed to me how Carlos had been sexually abusing her and Celeste, and how it all started. The grooming began when they were very young, about five and seven years old. When his plans for sexual gratification did not work as fast as he wanted, Carlos started shaming and punishing them for his own sick desires. Then he overpowered them physically and threatened each one into silent submission. Upon hearing Anne's story and knowing what Carlos had done to me, something broke loose inside my heart and I knew what needed to come next.

After first confirming that Carlos was asleep, I went into his room right next to the kitchen, found his .38 revolver in the dresser, put it into my pants' pocket, and ran across the house to find Anne again. I told her my intention to kill Carlos. She agreed and hugged me in clear affirmation.

Carlos was lying face up on the big green couch in the den. Anne and I walked very quietly across the green linoleum floor to the corner of the couch where his head was resting on a pillow. I tiptoed to within inches of his head. Anne was right behind me with her hand on my shoulder as I removed the revolver from my pocket, cocked it very quietly, stretched out my arm, and pointed the gun up to his head. After taking a deep breath, I pulled the trigger. No shot rang out. The hammer hit an empty chamber.

Anne yelled frantically, "Shoot him, shoot him, shoot him!" I tried desperately but the trigger was a hard pull, and I was so scared I could not even think to cock the revolver again. I would have killed him if I could.

With all the noise, Carlos woke up very startled and seized the gun from my right hand with his own right hand. Still lying down, he then grabbed me by the collar of my shirt with his left hand and pulled me closer to him. He was screaming, not in English or in Spanish, but with just an open mouthed scream. Anne yelled, "Let him go! Let him go!"

Carlos had the gun in his hand and I knew he was going to use it as a club on me. I prepared for the worst beating and thought he would surely kill me on the spot, just as I had intended to kill him. I wasn't at all prepared for what happened next.

Carlos stopped suddenly, frozen on the spot. I had never ever seen him frightened before. His face was pale and he broke out into a sweat. Then he released me, sat up slowly, almost mechanically, stood up, walked into his room, and closed the door. All the while he was shaking his head and talking unintelligibly to himself. It was the day I finally learned it was possible to stand up to bullies regardless of the consequences.

That was the last time Carlos ever beat or verbally degraded Celeste, Anne, or me. His abuse of the Teitelbaum children started in 1947, when we were eleven, seven, five, and three years old. I desperately wish it wasn't true, but although the beatings ceased after this incident, Carlos continued to sexually molest Celeste for many years thereafter.

One Safe Place

School was over for the year. It was decided that we could no longer live in the large ranch house because utilities were too expensive. We moved into the five-room house near the front of our property instead. Food continued to be scarce.

Mom eventually made arrangements for us to move to Beverly Hills, into our grandparents' home on La Peer Drive. She sold some of our household paintings, statues, and furniture since we needed money and Pop did not help at all with the finances anymore. The double Steinway piano was purchased by Walter Kirschner for $800. Mom stored the rest of our furniture in an empty house at the old Tower Ranch, courtesy of Kirschner.

Because of foreclosure proceedings, we only had 3 days notice to pack up what we could take with us to Beverly Hills, which amounted to a few pieces of furniture and some personal goods. All I took was a pillow, my clothes in two suitcases, and a few boxes of games. We filled a small rented trailer and drove away. Carlos took a truck full of furniture to use for himself, since he and Hannah were leaving for Los Angeles with their children, Claudia and Gerald, who were now 10 and 3 years old.

The urgency of our departure generated a great deal of speculation and more rumors all over town. My friends called me described how the stories had gone wild, fueled by our exit on a Friday night under a full moon. Celeste and Anne were reportedly insane witches. It was believed that I was chained under the refrigerator. Mom was known to be holding full moon séances, walking the compounds all night long, talking in strange languages, and shrieking in shrill tones. Everyone believed that the ghost of my sister, Linda, was haunting the property.

After I shared the rumors with Mom, she made a series of phone calls to her friends and to the Mayor. The lies and rumors immediately stopped.

I was heart broken because we could not take our dogs with us. Nicky had been in the family since my birth in Chicago. She had always been either at my side or in the compound. Carlos' family promised that they would take care of the dogs in our absence. Fred, Carlos' brother, later told me truth, though. The small dogs were given away. It was probably Nicky and Rufus' nightly howls that neighbors mistook as haunting cries. Our beloved dogs died from starvation on the property within three weeks of our departure.

Fred Martén gave me Rufus when I was a little boy, about five years old. He entrusted me with the half coyote mix and helped me name him. Rufus had reddish fur with a white chest. Fred told me that he found Rufus and Nicky's bones lying next to each other in the compound's dog pen. He was positive about their identity, because they still had collars around their skeleton necks. Approximately three years later Fred showed me where he buried them in the date groves, almost in the same spot where I buried Boy in 1954.

Beverly Hills

Mom, Anne, and I moved from Indio into our grandparents' home in the summer of 1958, located on a beautiful tree-lined quiet street. Yvonne DeCarlo resided there previously. It was a two-story apartment with a refrigerator and an icebox requiring the bi-weekly delivery of block ice. There were two large bedrooms, two bathrooms, and a spacious patio to serve us. Celeste returned to Indio to finish high school, staying with family friends in Mecca. Anne registered to attend Beverly Hills High School. I started the eighth grade at Horace Mann Junior High School in Beverly Hills.

I was the new kid on the block who dressed in a funny white T-shirt with a white pressed shirt on top, 501 jeans, and old wing tip shoes that my father left on the ranch after a visit. Looking like that, I had to work hard to be accepted. After a while, I found a few friends, but was not included in most social groups since they had grown up together and shared family experiences. They were quite cliquish and generally unwilling or unable to admit newcomers. I now know that this was merely an adolescent expression and not aimed directly at me, but at the time I was clearly affected by their alienating treatment. I was an outsider in a new school and definitely did not have the social skills to fit in until high school.

Grandfather Herman helped me study all summer. My thirteenth birthday fell on September 22, 1958, and I eagerly anticipated celebrating my Bar Mitzvah. Early that November my grandfather, Herman Melnick, a man I loved and respected, died at Mount Sinai Hospital from a combination of prostate cancer and surgical malpractice. There is only so much loss a person can take. I felt completely lost and believed that God had turned His back on me, so I stopped my religious studies altogether.

I survived middle school and moved on to Beverly Hills High School where I finally made a number of friends despite not having developed social graces over the years. Nonetheless, I was free from the grip of my main tormenter. Because he moved to a different city, Carlos was effectively removed from my life, at least in a physical manner. It would be many, many more years before I could begin the painful work of extricating his deeper toxic presence from my psyche. Meanwhile, I kept an eye out for entertaining distractions.

Circus Act

The summer after eighth grade I wandered around Hollywood and saw tents going up for the circus. The owner set up a whole series of tents at the Pan Pacific Auditorium Park across from Gilmore's drive-in movie lot.

I found out who the boss was and asked if I could carry water for the elephants, since I had so much skill from back home. He said that he couldn't pay me, so I asked to be compensated with tickets and he agreed. I started carrying water for the elephants and found out quickly that they liked to lean toward each other, like hugging cousins. A small boy of thirteen could get hurt when elephants leaned in, so I was taught how to use a bull prod to keep from being squeezed between them. Earning circus tickets made me popular, especially when I shared them with friends and family. I arrived at the fairway around ten in the morning, worked all day long, and shared a noon meal with all the roustabouts and performers. My day ended at six o'clock in the evening with a handful of entrance tickets to help fill the audience for the big top's main evening event.

Celeste and Anne were frequent recipients of tickets and Celeste dated my boss, the owner's nephew. He was a handsome man in his early thirties who was responsible for the entire circus. On Friday morning I was chosen to join a small group of people for a KCOP, Channel 13, interview about their world's tallest giraffe. We were filmed with the giraffe and it was a little thrilling to watch myself among the others on television at ten o'clock that night.

After two weeks I was asked to help with the world's largest brown bear. The bear cage had horizontal bars and long steel rods connected to ropes. When twenty men worked together, they created a web-like net out of the ropes and rods, corralling the bear in a corner of his cage. Then, they told me to get into the cage and sweep it out with a broom. That is when I quit working at the circus for good, that summer of 1957. I was naive but not stupid.

First Love

Even though I was no longer employed at the circus, over the next two weeks I made friends with a young lady contortionist. Kristi had blue eyes and could twist her body into a pretzel. She danced in skimpy costumes at the sideshow off the midway. I loved watching her and eventually she started talking to me. During my second circus week, Kristi invited me into her trailer. She had a small bedroom and her parents, also performers, lived in the other side of the trailer, so we went about our business quietly. Kristi was seventeen years old and liked to talk about everything. She was very funny and I fancied her. She guided me in sexual exploration far beyond anything a thirteen year-old child should know. We spent five nights together in her trailer and I learned to stifle my excited voice in a pillow.

Although I learned nothing about love or intimacy from our brief relationship, I did learn how two people could find comfort in each other's arms. Comfort was a rare commodity in my life up to that moment, and the lesson was not lost on me. Some of the mystery between men and women that I desired had also been revealed during our time together.

When the circus left town, Kristi kissed me, said goodbye, and headed down the highway. I felt neither love nor loss. Despite the comfort I received, something felt wrong about our relationship and there were no moral or ethical influences in my world to help sort through the experience. It was just another broken piece added to my difficult young life, which developed in a crazy-quilt pattern.

Pop's Death

My father was released from prison in August, 1975, after serving three years of a six months to life sentence for improper land transaction and non-distribution of a commission check. He had been in Chino's Elm Hall along with judges, attorneys, and various mob members like Jimmy Fratiani. The prison was anxious to release him, and pushed through an arrangement for Pop to work in my Studio City store under my supervision. Suffice it to say that Pop was not idle while in prison; his legal expertise continued to cause havoc within the prison system.

Once released, Pop's workweek at the store was Monday through Saturday. He invited the company of old friends to hang out at his new social center. Except for the mobsters' age, this could have been a satellite office for Chicago's Fine Arts building back in the early days. The tab that Pop and his aging friends ran up at Art's Deli across Ventura Boulevard was approximately $750.00 per week, which I covered.

My half-brother and I regularly provided Pop with spending money because he loved to share his money with others. By giving him a couple of hundred dollars at a time, we helped Pop maintain a small degree of self-respect and helped prevent his embarrassment. No matter how much we gave him, however, he always needed more within one or two days.

One of my father's old clients owned a well-known, worldwide chain of hotels based in Chicago. They gifted my father with a permanent suite in Beverly Hills on Beverly Drive. The tab was covered by services Pop rendered them over the past many years. He lived there for approximately three years. Steve and I tracked his daily whereabouts by paying all of Pop's taxi bills.

Abraham Teitelbaum died in 1980 in an airplane on his way to New York City. Pop always told me, "If you do something, make sure you do it big and that there are people around to notice." I guess he ended his life the way he lived it. Big!

After eating two pastrami sandwiches from Nate and Al's Deli in Beverly Hills, Pop boarded an airplane and had a fatal heart attack somewhere over New Mexico. The plane was forced to land in Albuquerque so his body could be removed. The whole event caused all of the passengers a great deal of distress.

That night my stepbrother called me, quite distraught. He could not face the fact that Pop was dead and refused to go retrieve his body. He asked that I take my half-sister to pick up our father's body from Albuquerque. It was intended that we bury him at Mount Sinai Cemetery in Burbank on Sunday since Jewish cemeteries are closed on Saturday.

We flew to New Mexico and returned to the Burbank airport with Pop's body stored in the plane's underbelly. The next day all of the first and second family members gathered together. We rode together in limos to Mount Sinai Cemetery and went to the Chapel on the Hill. The service was to be held at 11:30 in the morning.

When we entered the chapel, we were surprised to find that about ten older people were already grieving inside. They were seated in the front rows, wailing hysterically. None of us had ever seen these people before, so we backed up and exited the chapel to recheck the schedule. Sure enough, it was Pop's name and time on the signage, so we headed back into chapel together, intending to make sure that Pop was in the coffin. We walked up the aisle, peered in, and confirmed that it was Pop all right.

We were seated briefly before the wailers came over and introduced themselves to us amidst their tears. "Hello, I'm your older brother from New York City and these are your other brothers and sisters. Even though we never met before, we know all about you from Dad. He visited us in New York at least four times this last year".

With tears streaming down their faces, they fabricated outrageous stories about Pop's frequent and recent visits to New York City. Finally, I stood up and said, "Pop had no money. My father had no money. I know my own family and also Pop's second family very well but I never heard about a third family in New York City." I continued with, "Pop was in prison for about two years, and was released from Chino into my care and supervision. Pop had no money except for what my half-brother or I gave him." I also told them I did not believe their story about Pop visiting them, since we always knew exactly what he was doing and where, and because we paid for all Pop's expenses. I thanked them for being there.

Aunt Ilana, now 77 years old, concluded this bizarre event by chirping in and calling out to the visitors, loud enough for all family and friends to hear, "I can tell a Teitelbaum when I see him. Just drop your pants!" Mom chuckled knowingly at Ilana's obnoxious statement, which may have been the only bonding moment which ever occurred between the two of them. If only we knew the historical threads leading to that shared laughter.

After the services we went to the gravesite and none of the supposed family members showed up. Mom and Aunt Ilana still had nothing good to say to each other but they agreed on what may be another singular occasion in their history, the interlopers were only looking for some nonexistent money.

I always wished Pop could have been a good father to me. He bragged to others that I could take care of myself, which excused him from any fatherly obligation to me. His gratitude for my support in those last years was clear, but his fatherly support was nonetheless nonexistent.

Mom's Death

Esther Teitelbaum passed away in 1995. When my sisters and I went through the contents of Mom's dresser, we found our sister, Linda's, personal items stored neatly in one of the drawers, just as though they were still in use. There was a hairbrush with Linda's hair still in it, Linda's clothing, socks, and other similar objects. We placed each of these keep-sakes at Mom's right side in the casket, which was interred in the mausoleum, about two hundred feet away from dear little Linda. Because of her young death, Linda was the only one of Mom's five children who had not experienced ongoing abuse.

I always believed that Mom was grieving for the loss of Linda and her great love, Pop. Now I stand corrected. There was no collection of memorial objects from Pop in our mother's dresser, just evidence that the loss of her daughter, Linda, was the most difficult experience and the greatest sorrow in Mom's life. Like Mom, each of us continues to grieve not only for Linda, but also for the unfathomable burdens of losing innocence, love, safety, beauty, respect, honesty, and hope.

Chapter Fourteen: Conclusion

When my ancestors were threatened with genocide, one brave woman, Frieda Rachel Lee Wasserman, foresaw the dangers and found a way to shepherd her loved ones to safety. They all thrived in this new environment through hard work, determination, and the blessings afforded by education in the sciences, humanities, and law.

I'm sorry to say that my parents used their legal education to help criminals prosper. They indulged in hedonistic, greedy, and deadly mischief during their early legal careers, which eventually led to untold suffering both inside and outside of their immediate family. My parents' agent, an immoral warlord, did his best to annihilate the bright light that was the Teitelbaum children's birthright.

Frieda was inspired to protect her loved ones from external threats and her farsighted clarity ensured our family's survival. After their migration to the United States, family stories emphasized the importance of seeing and interpreting faraway dangers. Whether because of this heritage, their own internal wiring, or a combination of the two, my parents in particular lost their ability to identify, correctly interpret, or even care about dangers closer to home. Those disabilities caused many lifetimes of grief for their descendants.

Internal threats must also be identified and addressed, by calling the name of each danger out loud for all to hear, and taking a stand for corrective action.

Post Script

Separating from my family of origin and neutralizing years of internalized rage continue to be life-long struggles. Just like my parents, I looked for external remedies to internal problems. I didn't really fit into the elite Beverly Hills high school culture but later found the Marine Corp to offer the most comforting structure and focus I had ever known. I married my sweetheart and then regressed by turning a grocery store receiving job into a variety of lucrative deals that would have made my father proud.

To reduce the rage that seemed to consume me, I indulged in a wide variety of anesthetizing street drugs, which eventually took a tremendous toll on my heart and forced me to acknowledge my own mortality. Like Pop, I tended to live larger than my means, as though I had more resources than I actually did.

In 1993, Carol and I joined Riverside County's "Prevent Child Abuse Council," hoping to make a difference in the lives of children in the Coachella Valley, where my family resided. In 2006, Carol was asked to join others in research about the under-reporting of abused boys. Carol then created the "It Happens to Boys" project and introduced me to other male survivors and experts in the field of trauma abuse and recovery. I became acquainted with courageous men of all ages who accepted and supported me. This was the beginning of my recovery process. Once we began presenting the "It Happens to Boys" conferences, I met the best-selling author and speaker, Dave Pelzer. I have taken his story to heart. Dave said, "No matter what happens to you in your childhood, you can heal and become a productive member of society." Now I am pleased to count Dave as my friend. Because of our conferences I have also been fortunate to meet John Bradshaw and John Lee, two other deeply inspirational men from whom I have learned a great deal.

Recovery from child abuse is much like recovering from drugs and alcohol; it must be done one day at a time. Let the truth be known; no one is ever recovered, we are all recovering. I am still triggered by demonic memories periodically, but now I have tools to deal with those demons.

Unlike my parents, I love and have always loved, even when I retaliated against my uncaring environment. My story's joyful canine cast is probably largely responsible for the preservation of my empathic nature.

The greatest family joys in my childhood were occasions when we shared stories. They were always lovely stories, triumphant successes, or humorous anecdotes. The truth is that stories are not always pretty, which makes them nonetheless generous contributions to loved ones. Cautionary tales, epiphanies, dangers, and sorrows are all gifts.

Some say that life is like a train; a metaphor that I believe has merit. My family life was more like the thick metal spikes that hold railroad ties in place so that life, be it rough or smooth, can move forward. My immediate family was a painful necessity born of vision and greed, involving hard labor, sweat, and death.

Now life's horizon, in contrast to the past, is populated with true friends, beauty, honesty, love, and great joy. After my hurricane childhood, I see splendid sunsets within reach, with extravagant clouds and abundant, beautiful, deep colors greeting me. If this book is at all helpful, your own stories will not have to wait sixty-eight years in the telling, as mine did.

"Potato Latkes"

Melnick family recipe dating back to 1850

Stories are important to the Melnicks, my maternal family. We sit around and swap memories at any occasion that finds us together. We tell stories, exchange jokes, retell events of importance, and even share recipes that help tie us together; how we love to cook and eat. Not unlike most families I know, stories, even those retold over and over, reinforce the very fabric of what makes us family.

From my great-great-grandparents and parents, stories are passed from generation to generation. Now I pass them on to my kids and grandchildren freely so they know, without regret, where they come from. One of my favorite family narrative traditions to pass on is a recipe said to come directly from Great-Great-Grandmother Freda Rachel Leah Wasserman, to her daughter, to my grandmother to my very own mother for potato latkes, a traditional dish served around the Jewish holiday, Chanukah. It seems we are 'commanded' to eat fried food at that time of year. Of course, latkes can be eaten at any time of year. I recently taught my daughter, Dawn, and grand-daughters, Paris and Paloma, how to make the traditional Melnick latkes, knowing full well they will teach their children the very same recipe I taught them.

4	Medium to large potatoes
4	Large brown onions (Maui Sweet Onions are best)
2	Eggs
4	Tablespoons of all-purpose flour
1/10	Teaspoon of baking power
	Corn oil
2	Tablespoons butter

Peel onions and potatoes
Shred the onions and potatoes
Mix onions and potatoes together evenly, including any juice
Add the eggs and all-purpose flour
Add baking power
Again mix well

In a heavy skillet, use ¼ inch of corn oil and add 2 tablespoons of butter
Heat the oil, stirring in the butter
Once the oil is hot enough for frying, use an ice cream scoop size of the mixture
Place mixture in the center of skillet
Add 7 more scoops
Do not turn too often to avoid excess oiliness. Keep the darkest side up.

When cooked thoroughly remove from pan. Drain excess oil by placing latkes on paper towels and salt to taste or use your favorite spices.

Enjoy my secret family recipe with your own family!

Additional Resources

Website: www.Frogsandsnailsandmobstertales.com

Made in the USA
Charleston, SC
17 October 2015